THE ORACLE CREATOR

The Modern Guide to Creating an Oracle or Tarot Deck

First published in 2021 by Liminal 11.

Graphic Designers: Tori Jones, Allie Oldfield, Gill Ha and Jing Lau
Editor: Eleanor Treemer
Editorial Director: Darren Shill
Art Director: Kay Medaglia

With special thanks to Loveday May.

Printed in China

ISBN 978-1-912634-35-4

10 9 8 7 6 5 4 3 2 1

www.liminal11.com

Contents Pages

INTRODUCTION

For as long as there have been human beings, we have used whatever means we have to try and tell the future. Evolving from using the reflection of clouds in pools of water to shuffling decks of cards, the oracle has remained popular, even as the world changes. People have always found an interest in the unseen hand of fate and discovering what might lie in their future. And I am no exception.

My own experience of oracles goes back over 25 years to when I happened upon a pack of tarot cards in a supermarket here in the UK. This is not, I might add, the romantic or magical introduction to the art of the oracle that I may have wished for — but it did open the door to an inspired life and, eventually, a career.

Yet I have realized, on reflection, that my interest in the oracle goes back further still. As a child, I would trace the raindrops on my window, making up stories based around the twists and turns they'd take as they made their way down. Laying my fate in one of two, I'd watch in anticipation. If the raindrop stopped dead, then my hopes would be dashed. If it joined forces with another and raced to the bottom of the pane, then I'd consider my wish acknowledged. The faster the raindrop, the sooner my question would be successfully answered. Of course, I wasn't aware that I was consulting an oracle of sorts, but my fascination with fortune telling remained. And yet, I had not expressed an interest in tarot until that Friday afternoon in north London. I gave the cover of the box a once-over and popped it into my supermarket trolly.

The purchase of my first tarot deck planted a seed. As much as the process of divination intrigued and excited me, the many ways in which artists design their packs was of equal interest. I was mesmerized by the different artworks, and, as with many tarot enthusiasts, readers and commentators, I eventually created my own tarot pack. In 2017, my *Spirit Within Tarot* deck was released by Schiffer Publishing. Beginning as a series of illustrations for my online teachings (which were created to avoid breaching the copyright of the famous *Rider-Waite-Smith Tarot*), the images became of interest to those viewing my work and people started asking where they could get a set. I was not entirely sure how to go about publishing a deck back then. After approaching a few well-known companies, I was fortunate that Schiffer liked what they saw and took a punt on me. I'm pleased to say that the deck is still enjoying much success, is regularly spotted on the shelves of bookshops around the world and has been fanned across the tables of many inspiring readers and teachers.

Page Right: Photography by Bright, S. Card from *The Luna Sol Tarot*, Medaglia, K. and Shill, D.

That's just my story. People create oracles for many different reasons and in many different ways. In this book I'll be exploring all the different forms oracles can take — and I'll talk you through some of the ways in which you can bring the deck in your head (or heart, perhaps) to life.

This book includes...

- A step-by-step guide on how to create your own oracle
- Exercises that encourage you to develop your ideas
- An overview of the various oracle systems that exist, and instructions on how to create your own system
- Annotated oracle cards and deck examples
- A directory of symbols and symbolic color meanings
- Exclusive interviews from industry insiders
- A guide on how to publish your deck

With tips and tricks passed on by those who have published their own oracles, we'll examine the different methods of creating an oracle or tarot deck, as well as finding an approach for varying types of artistic ability and budget.

Although not everybody will want to sell their work, there are more ways of getting your oracle into print than ever before; you'll find a wealth of information from publishers and self-published creators here. You may have wondered: What do publishers look for in a new deck or expect from a proposal? How do you start a Kickstarter campaign? What are the pros and cons of self-publishing? If so, you will find your answers within this book.

As a writer, I have heard on many occasions that 'there is a book within all of us'. I believe this to be true, since every human being — whether they have the inclination to write or not — has their own wealth of experience and personal perspective to share. For you, that 'book within' may actually be an oracle deck.

In recent years, social media platforms such as Instagram have provided us with an opportunity to express ourselves in pictures more so than words. In sentences littered with emojis, we can quickly comprehend a mood or someone's state of mind. For a generation of people so used to communicating through images — from the magnificent to the mundane — the oracle is a perfect way to share our personal perspective of the world and divine our place within it.

CONSIDERING AN ORACLE

Contents

THE FIRST ORACLES

Divination is not new. The techniques may have changed over time, and while many of our questions can now be answered scientifically, the desire to catch a glimpse of *something* outside our realm of reality is as strong now as it has ever been. Growth in technology has altered our lives monumentally, but many of us recognize that some of our innate, intuitive skills have been lost — or, at the very least, subdued. This is why the renewed interest in tarot, and other tools that can help restore the balance between intellect and intuition, has grown up in response to technological advancement. But if we really want to understand the roots of divination, and the connection with human intuition, we have to go back to the start.

Shamanism is one of the world's earliest religious traditions — and is probably the earliest form of divination. A tradition dating back to the Paleolithic era, a shaman is someone who is able to enter into a state of trance and can, through ritual, make contact with the spirit world to divine reasons behind sickness and offer natural healing. The casting and reading of stones and bones are methods of ancient shamanic divination and are still practiced today. The questions have most probably changed, since we now have more reliable means of predicting the weather or locating our next meal, but some of these natural tools and practices have survived and are regaining popularity. Many modern practitioners will still divine answers from the clouds overhead, pools of water, or the flickering embers in a fire.

Divination has been common throughout history, from the more famous oracles to roadside fortune telling. One of the most well-known sites for divination is in Greece. The temple of Delphi is known for its priestesses, who served as oracles and messengers of Apollo. Often depicted holding snakes, these women would receive important information from the great deity. It is said that the philosopher Socrates consulted the oracles at Delphi. The Roman emperors also employed soothsayers and haruspices as advisors, and this practice was common for rulers across the ancient world.

But divination was also practiced by everyday folk — those wishing to know the odds of going to war, the prospects of a marriage, or whether a voyage would be successful or not. Often, this divination didn't rely on rune-tossing or entrail-inspecting, but on the simple observation of natural phenomenon, known as omens. The flight of birds, streaks of lightning, or oddities in livestock births were all considered omens, thought to reflect the events that were about to occur. And this belief in omens still persists in parts of the world today.

So, if there are so many types of divination, why is it that card reading is the most popular? We can thank the Romani people for that. The practice of fortune-telling has long been associated with the Roma, listed as a cultural occupation from as early as 1422 in Belgium and Italy and 1414 in France and Germany. The skills of palmistry, tea leaf reading, and cartomancy were passed down from the Roma women to their daughters, and there were three styles of reading acknowledged: the lofty, the familiar, and the homely. These different ways of giving readings were dependent on the rank of person being read for, and the fortune teller knew how to adapt their style for different clients. It is largely because of the Roma, whose nomadic lifestyle took them to many different countries, that card reading is perhaps the most popular form of divination.

THE HISTORY OF CARTOMANCY

The use of cards as an oracle, which we will mainly concentrate on in this book, has a shorter history. Playing cards have been used as a fortune-telling device for centuries; Mamluk cards, for instance, were brought to Western Europe from Turkey in the 14th Century. Predominantly used for gaming, many of these card decks are the forerunners of what we see today. But of course, the most well-known type of divination deck is the tarot.

The tarot is most often associated with fortune telling, but many practitioners use it for brainstorming, creative storytelling, and self-reflection. Containing 22 trump cards and 56 suited cards (similar to the humble playing card deck), the tarot is a mirror of our physical, mental, and emotional world, encouraging us to identify and engage with its many scenarios and plots.

The tarot has been used for divination since the Renaissance, though any roots stretching back before then are veiled in mystery. Originating in the Mediterranean, what we know as tarot was first called *tarocchi*. One of the earliest decks (first editions of which now reside in libraries and private collections) dates back to 1451. As a tenth wedding anniversary gift for his wife, Francesco Sforza hired the artist Bonafacio Bembo to create a deck of cards in honor of the occasion. The result was the luxurious *Visconti-Sforza Tarot*, painted in gold leaf and depicting what are thought to be images of Bianca Maria and Francesco. Descendants of these

Italian card decks began to pop up elsewhere, notably in France. The less lavishly illustrated *Tarot de Marseille* was widely distributed and used for gaming and gambling. The earliest designs of the *Marseille* cards originated in 1650.

The origins of tarot have been much debated, and although many occult groups have claimed that tarot tradition goes back to ancient magical practices, there's not much historical evidence to support this. However, considering that cartomancy was growing in popularity at about the time that the first tarocchi decks were in circulation, it's likely that even early on they were being used for divinatory purposes. In the late 18th Century, Jean-Baptiste Alliette was one of the first to link the tarot to astrology and numerology, believing that the cards themselves originated in Egypt. It was Alliette (or Etteilla, as he was better known) who created the first tarot deck especially for divination.

It was in the 20th Century that tarot really took off, thanks in large part to the *Rider-Waite-Smith Tarot* (directed by Edward Arthur Waite and illustrated by Pamela Colman Smith) which was first published in 1909 by William Rider & Son and remains most widely known today. Most tarots either follow this pattern, that of the *Marseille*, or of *The Thoth Tarot* (conceived by Aleister Crowley, painted by Lady Frida Harris, and published in 1969). But not all card deck oracles follow the tarot structure. Some, such as the Lenormand, have their own specifications. Made popular by Mademoiselle Marie Anne Lenormand in the later part of the 18th Century, these decks have just 36 cards, and people are still creating new decks using this system today.

In present times, the use of the oracle deck has broadened and mirrors the kind of people purchasing and using them. While the oracles of old have been given modern twists and have therefore been adapted to suit the trends of our age, we have also seen the growth of packs that provide a more affirmative voice. Made popular by New Age writers, Angel cards have grown in popularity and elbowed many of the other oracles off mainstream bookshelves. While Angel cards do vary in design, the most recognizable have soft illustrations with a paragraph or sentence of text below, providing uplifting, positive guidance. Mostly used as a daily pick-up or as part of high-vibe and empowering readings, this genre of oracle has exploded in recent years. To cater to their customers, publishers have also incorporated fairies, unicorns, and magical beings such as mermaids into their oracular family.

The world of oracle card decks is as varied as its inhabitants. There are more decks being produced today than ever before, and the rules for cartomancy (if there actually are any) have changed considerably. You could argue that anything goes when it comes to creating an oracle deck — which leaves the door wide open for a designer's creativity.

Page Left: Photography by May, L. Cards from *Modern Witch Tarot*, Sterle, L.

WHY DO PEOPLE CREATE ORACLES?

LILY OF THE VALLEY

WISTERIA

TULIP

HENBANE

BLUEBELL

An oracle can become a reflective and helpful tool, so it's important that the deck both serves your needs and mirrors your personal ethics and tastes. With this in mind, some come to the art of oracle designing with a need to create a deck that is close to their heart, but which cannot be found on the bookstore shelves — I myself have put decks back on the shop shelf simply because I didn't like the way a specific card had been rendered. So, what are your main reasons for creating your own deck?

Surrounding: *The Seed and Sickle Oracle Deck,* Inkwright, F.

DAISY

OAK

BRAMBLE

BELLADONNA

MISTLETOE

CREATIVITY

An oracle deck can give form to a series of art pieces. Because all cards relate to one another simply by being in the same deck, they are both individual and part of the collective. The creation of a series of images for divination can be a great way of setting off an artist's creativity. Just the card systems themselves can spark inspiration: how a designer interprets every card, even each archaic symbol, in their own artistic style can be deeply personal.

Not everyone who creates a deck of cards comes from a card reading background, though. In recent years, divinatory card systems have become a unique vehicle to showcase the work of artists who have not previously encountered cartomancy. A sizable deck can act as a portfolio, enabling art lovers and enthusiasts to own an affordable body of work. Therefore, it is a perfect way of distributing and marketing your creative pursuits, should you wish to share them.

SPIRITUALITY

Of course, many others design oracle decks specifically as a spiritual tool. Some people may wish to use their oracle as a way of connecting to a specific deity or higher consciousness, and the cards can be an effective way of doing so. Other artists use decks to explore various mythologies or pagan cultures, while some design decks to be used specifically as part of magical practice. Not everyone will find what they are looking for spiritually, however, and building your own oracle could be a way around this.

Oracle cards can be used for more than just reading about our daily lives, too; some people place them on their altars or use their messages for spiritual growth. There are decks that have been produced to help guide us through the shadows of life or assist our connection with different realms. Mediumship, as an example, has been the subject of a variety of oracles, using the cards as a tool for connecting with those who have passed.

PERSONAL REPRESENTATION

An oracle is supposed to reflect the life of the person reading it or those being read for, so if someone picks up a deck and doesn't see themselves represented, this can feel alienating. While there is far more diversity in the world of oracle decks than before, we still have a way to go before everyone feels included. If you do not see yourself represented in existing decks, it could be your aim to rectify that: to create something for your social group, or just as a personal tool that better reflects your experiences.

The artist and Shamanic healer Maryam Elen Jones created her Voices of the Dark Mothers oracle cards after having difficulty in finding a goddess-themed deck that

she could relate to. "The decks I found always showed young, conventional-looking whitewomen but never displayed older women, or addressed people who didn't identify as a woman," she says. "I felt like they reinforced stereotypes and probably didn't help people who might have body image issues from looking at such images."

Feeling perturbed by this, Elen set about creating her own oracle deck, featuring a wide array of body shapes, ages, and cultures. In many of the images, the goddesses are gender-ambiguous, focusing mainly on their energy or backstory, meaning that the deck would suit a variety of users. While this oracle identifies a gap in the market, it is also an invaluable tool for the artist who created it. "I felt inspired to try to create something different," she says.

DIVERSITY

If you are designing with the consumer in mind, it is important to remember that your work will be available to a great deal of people. This is something worthy of great consideration because not everyone buying a tarot or oracle deck will be just like you. People come from different cultures and backgrounds, and not all of us look alike; our abilities vary, as will our sexual preferences and lifestyles. Whether you choose to acknowledge this in your work is your choice, but many modern designers are focusing on making divination tools as inclusive and accessible as possible. But how do you represent an experience that is outside your own?

When considering the subject of diversity, the most important thing to remember is to be respectful. If you are depicting someone from a cultural background, religion or lifestyle different to your own, sensitivity and authenticity is key. A mistake arising from lack of research could risk offending those very people you intended to honor. Thankfully, we live in an era in which information is at our very fingertips. My rule of thumb is this: if you are in any doubt as to how to depict someone who appears to be different to yourself, consult with those people who might be able to offer insight from experience. And try not to go for the obvious: while it might make sense to you to depict *The Chariot* as a wheelchair-user, think about why this figure would be just as appropriate for any of the other 77 cards in the tarot deck. Or even more than one!

HEALING

The creation of an oracle deck can also help artists work through grief or share ways in which others might cope with pain. The *Pearls of Wisdom Tarot* by Roxi Sim is a good example of such a deck. When asked what inspired her first tarot project, she says: "I had lost my health and my son to Lyme disease, and my mother to cancer… you could say I was beyond depressed." As an experienced art teacher, Roxi took to painting as a method of healing after her son's death. It was upon returning from Grenada that her mother passed away and her depressive state went from bad to worse. People suggested that Roxi's new artworks resembled tarot cards, which is

The Devil

where the interest in creating a deck originated from. "I painted what I needed to see — bright colours, uplifting images," she says. "I put my attention into creating, rather than grieving, though I never stopped the tears that came as I painted."

With a history in art therapy, Roxi used the process of deck-creating a second time. After further losses within her family, including the loss of her home, she set to work on an oracle, The Sacred Feminine. "With no space of my own, I worked on my lap, using colored pencils. I recreated paintings I'd completed in the past as part of my art therapy and wrote guided meditations for health, wellbeing, and self-care to accompany them." Once again, the colors were vibrant and the mood uplifting. Since creating this second deck, Roxi has been treated for Lyme disease and her health has improved greatly.

Both deck designing and card reading can have a therapeutic benefit. The former allows someone to unburden themselves and reflect on their life's experiences. Reading an oracle can provoke an inner dialogue or inspire conversation between reader and client, sparking understanding and emotional release. Specific oracles have been built with this in mind, such as the *Healing Grief Card Deck* by David Kessler. Remembering that grief is evidence of love, his card system contains 55 practices to help find peace after loss, one card at a time.

TAUNI LOVE
Creator of the *Tarot Magnus*

What specific need did you have for creating your own deck?

I created my homemade tarot deck in the winter of 2011. I had started to gradually lose my eyesight the previous summer, and my regular go-to decks had become difficult to use; larger decks worked, but they were cumbersome. I needed a regular sized deck, with minimal imagery and enough contrast for me to discern the symbols. I couldn't find one like that, so I decided to make one. The distraction actually helped me to cope with what turned out to be a very stressful two years as I went between medical appointments, attempting to figure out why my eyes were failing.

What was your method for creating the deck and how did you produce it?

I used a pack of blank tarot cards from U.S. Games and a couple of sharpies. I kept it non-pictorial to keep the imagery uncluttered. The court cards required more consideration. I wanted them to be more universal and current than the traditional royal titles. I also needed names that could be individually represented with a different letter of the alphabet — for example, Knight and King, both starting with "K", wouldn't work. Ultimately, I chose Child (C) for Pages, Warrior (W) for Knights, Healer (H) for Queens, and Sage (S) for Kings. I chose these archetypes because they are relatable roles that we all experience — or aspire to experience — and they are also gender neutral and non-hierarchical. I didn't realize how much any of that mattered to me until I had to figure it out for my own deck.

The whole process took about seven weeks; I finished the last card a week before Christmas in 2011. But when I was done with drawing all of the symbols, I had a set of very white cards with bold black marks on them, and the glaring white really bothered my eyes. So, a couple of days before New Year's Eve, I tea-stained each card, and that was the final touch the deck needed.

My deck, in that form, was my reading partner for the next year and a half. Then, in June of 2013, it was finally confirmed that the shunt in my spine was shattered and I needed a new one. I had surgery for a new shunt in July of 2013 — two years almost to the day after I first started losing my eyesight. The new shunt restored some of the vision in my right eye, enough that my homemade deck looked kind of bland to me. So, that's when I added the keywords, in order to fill in some of that blank space. I noticed that taking my time to carefully choose each word helped me to bond with my deck even more.

COMPLETENESS
Return
achievement
destiny
fulfilled
Realization of Self
ONENESS
Finish Line
FULL CIRCLE
Success
right action

XXI

A Surge of Energy

10

Enthusiasm

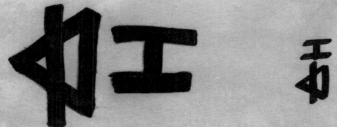

pure comfort

The Hostess

What has been the benefit of creating your own deck?

I initially had to resist giving up the project several times as my vision was declining rapidly, but ultimately it turned out to be an extremely healing and meaningful experience. Creating my own deck significantly deepened my relationship with tarot — not just the physical tool, but tarot as an energetic force. It has also increased my already immense respect for the numerous deck creators whose names I'm proud to have in my collection. My homemade deck, made without pictures, introduced me to those beautiful [tarot] images that I've accumulated within my consciousness. It's ironic how going blind made me realize what I could really see.

Were there any problems you faced when creating it?

My blindness occurred because my spinal shunt from 20 years prior had failed. However, it took two years for my doctors to figure that out. By the time the broken shunt was confirmed, most of my optic nerves were permanently damaged. I started to notice eye problems by July of 2011 and by the time I decided to create my deck, my vision was frequently inconsistent. I would be able to see for an hour or so, but then my eyesight would fade into complete darkness, like someone was playing with the overhead dimming lights in a ballroom. When things went dark, I'd have to stop what I was doing and wait a bit until I could see again.

So, whenever I was creating a card, with sharpie in hand, I had to be very focused and careful — but I also had to work somewhat swiftly, before everything went black. I could only do so much at a time because it was exhausting. Even with two eyes that could see, I could never draw a stick figure to save my life, but tarot is my passion, and the notion of not having it in my life broke my heart, so I just had to work around my lack of eyesight or art skills. Fortunately, in my case, the more minimalist the better, so I didn't need to make actual art or spend a huge amount of time on each card.

What advice would you give to anyone considering creating their own deck?

Don't strive for perfection, or you'll never finish your deck. Or rather, redefine perfection by creating your deck, your way, and to the best of your ability. Also, do very thorough research. Be solidly grounded in the symbolism you choose for your deck. Hold a vision but be willing to bend and stretch with it. And don't give up if something doesn't work: pause, regroup, and try something else.

Practically speaking, stock up on materials before you dive in, so you don't run out while you're within the flow of creativity. Enjoy the process: that phase is a bonding experience unique to the creation of one's own spiritual tool, and it shouldn't be missed.

Finally, know what you're getting yourself into, because it is quite an undertaking. I'm still amazed at how fascinated people are with my cards. As far as I'm concerned, I just filled a need, but apparently that's no small thing.

RELAXATION

Many have recognized the connection between creating art and better mental health. When we create something, such as an oracle deck, our mind and imagination are stimulated. When we become engaged with the process, it can help to push worries or anxieties aside. In recent years, there has been a big trend for coloring books aimed at adults and you can find them in many mainstream outlets in the UK, such as supermarkets. While they provide an obvious channel for creativity, the underlying purpose of an adult's coloring book is stress relief.

When choosing to color an image, we encounter a series of different problems to solve and the results of such can be rewarding. As with the creation of an oracle deck, there is no definitive answer, so individuality and creative thinking are wholly encouraged. The achievement of creating a piece of art can boost confidence, motivation and self-esteem.

FOR FUN

While there are many deep and meaningful reasons for creating an oracle, the one that most creators will identify with is the joy of doing so. Building an oracle can be a little like creating your own world: a place where your imagination has no limits and anything is possible. If you wish to design a tool based around a personal interest — let's say plants — then the study of botany and the spiritual meanings of flowers are at your finger-tips. Should you want to base your deck on architecture, a favourite place, or a favourite movie, the world is your oyster: though the latter may encounter issues of copyright should you wish to sell it… but more about that later.

Page Right:
Modern Witch Tarot, Sterle, L.
The Cosmic Slumber Tarot, Walden, T.
White Numen: A Sacred Animal Tarot. Gonzalez, A.

Is an Oracle Only Built With Cards?

The simple answer to this question is 'no'. An oracle can be made from just about anything. While the main focus of this book is the creation of a card deck, there are many other tools available for divination. Let's take a look at some of the more popular ones.

RUNES

The word 'rune' derives from the Gothic 'runa', which can be translated to mean a mystery or secret. Once the sacred alphabet of Germanic people in northern Europe, the runes are a popular choice for many wishing for an ancient form of divination. However, rather than being presented in card form (though some modern versions of rune cards exist), you will most commonly find the symbolic alphabet carved into wood or drawn onto stones.

The oldest complete runic alphabet is the Elder Futhark, and it comprises 24 symbols. Due to the evolution of language and the people using them, the runes were altered and added to over time. The Younger Futhark has just 16 runes, whereas the Northumbrian Futhark increased to 33. The Elder Futhark, incorporating runes relating to the seasons of the year, compass directions, and the hours of the day, has 36.

These days you will find many rune sets available, ranging from those molded in plastic for mass-marketing to individually crafted sets made from gemstones and crystals. Regardless of the many unique and attractive runes on sale, it is often suggested that the best set for an individual to use is the one they have made themselves. Some practitioners will hand-paint pebbles they have found, others will find a fallen branch from a tree and cut it into small disks before carving the runic symbols into each one.

Although we are looking at the process of creating cards in this book, it would be quite easy to apply what you read here to a set of runes. There are a variety of different runic alphabets to choose from but many have taken up the challenge of inventing their own. The process of planning, designing and publishing a set of runes is not unlike that of an oracle deck, whether you create an individual set for yourself or look into ways in which you might build sets for sale and mass-distribution.

CHARM CASTING

Charm casting has become very popular over the last decade or so. Charms (usually bought to add to bracelets) are concealed within a pouch, shaken, and a small handful are then dropped onto a cloth that has been created for this purpose, with specific sections drawn out on it to act as positions. The charms are randomly chosen, and where they fall on the layout of the cloth is the basis of the reading.

There are many inexpensive charms available for purchase, sometimes comprising of hundreds of different symbols. Most will offer a wide array of interesting potential meanings (see Symbol Directory, page 99). Alternatively, you could create your own charm set and choose the symbols you wish to read from.

JUNK ORACLE

The junk oracle is not dissimilar to those created with charms. Rather than consisting of only jewelry pieces, the junk oracle can be made up of just about anything. You can throw in button-badges, a safety pin, a ring, key, thimble, hook, battery, a child's tooth, dice, a padlock, or even a lost piece from a jigsaw puzzle. There really are no rules when it comes to a junk oracle and most of us will be able to find things at home to start a healthy collection.

A junk oracle is used in much the same way as a charm casting set. While a reading mat or cloth is not essential, it can make reading that bit more effective. Although some cloths will be ornately designed, a makeshift template can be put together quickly with a sizable piece of paper. Some junk readers will ask their seeker to pull one or two items from the oracle bag. With this in mind, it makes sense to put together a selection of pieces that are similar in size and weight so that they are not immediately identifiable when being drawn.

PLANNING YOUR ORACLE

Contents

The success of an oracle deck is very much dependent on its usability. While an oracle can incorporate all of the required components (such as a title, image, keywords, numbering, and a back design), this does not necessarily deem it successful. Choosing the right titles and images takes time and should not be hurried. Planning is an underrated part of the process.

First and foremost: you must decide what your oracle deck will be used for. If you are envisioning that it will be used for romantic readings, the cards will look quite different to a deck created for questions around business and career. If, like most designers, you wish for your cards to address a multitude of different questions, the cards must be flexible enough to encompass many areas of life. Therefore, the most sensible first step is to plan out what cards are needed to ensure that all possible outcomes or responses are included.

In this chapter, we will go through the planning of an oracle deck, step by step, working out which kind of cards would make for a well-rounded and effective divination tool. Every reading will need cards that suggest fresh starts, describe the ins-and-outs of a situation and conclude the narrative in one way or another. A good oracle reading is, after all, a story — and the cards must fit into the framework of this.

GETTING STARTED

THE MAGICIAN

THE HERMIT

THE EMPEROR

EIGHT *of* CUPS

PAGE *of* PENTACLES

KNIGHT *of* SWORDS

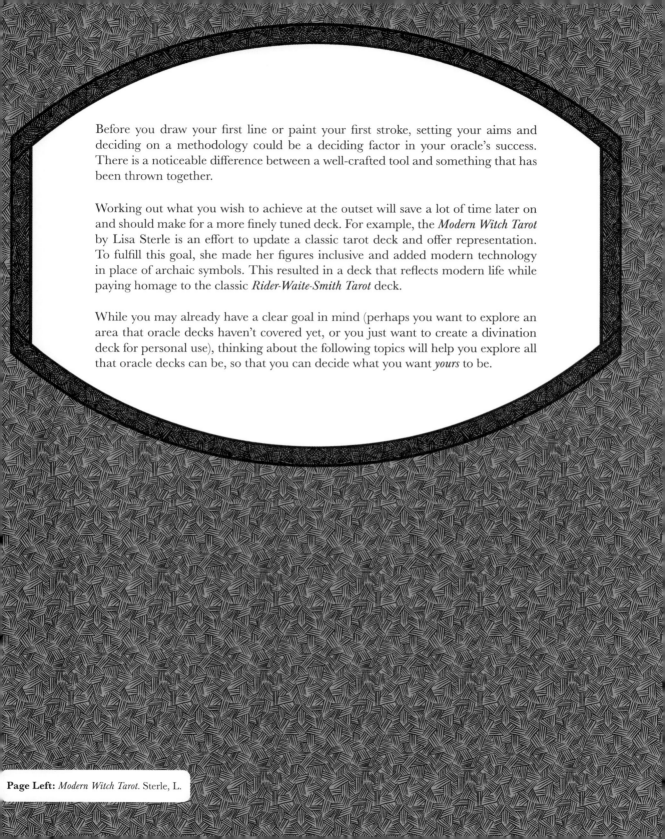

Before you draw your first line or paint your first stroke, setting your aims and deciding on a methodology could be a deciding factor in your oracle's success. There is a noticeable difference between a well-crafted tool and something that has been thrown together.

Working out what you wish to achieve at the outset will save a lot of time later on and should make for a more finely tuned deck. For example, the *Modern Witch Tarot* by Lisa Sterle is an effort to update a classic tarot deck and offer representation. To fulfill this goal, she made her figures inclusive and added modern technology in place of archaic symbols. This resulted in a deck that reflects modern life while paying homage to the classic *Rider-Waite-Smith Tarot* deck.

While you may already have a clear goal in mind (perhaps you want to explore an area that oracle decks haven't covered yet, or you just want to create a divination deck for personal use), thinking about the following topics will help you explore all that oracle decks can be, so that you can decide what you want *yours* to be.

Page Left: *Modern Witch Tarot.* Sterle, L.

HOW DO YOU WANT YOUR ORACLE TO BE USED?

You will need to consider how you wish others to use your deck — or how you would like to use it if you don't intend to publish. Some decks can be used in a variety of different ways, but there are others which are geared toward a specific style of reading; trying to use them in ways that diverge from that can be a little like trying to squeeze two non-matching pieces of a jigsaw puzzle together.

The *Original Angel Cards* by Kathy Tyler and Joy Drake were invented as tokens for daily inspiration. Containing just a word and a very small illustration (secondary to the text), these pocket-sized rectangular cards can be used for divinatory readings if you desire, but they are more often used to provoke thought and self-reflection. A card such as Relaxation, which shows a simplistic hammock stretched above the elaborately handwritten text, could advise that you need to take some rest.

Inspiration cards such as these could also be used for meditation. Pulling a card such as *Purpose* can act as a prompt, provoking you to meditate on the direction of your own life, what your goals are and where you want to end up. Although the card does not provide an answer or solution, it can act as a reminder to check in with yourself. Some people enjoy pulling a card from a deck like this on a daily basis so that they can ponder the chosen concept throughout the day. It can be enlightening when that same word then appears in a magazine advert or on the radio, confirming that this is certainly something you need to be thinking about!

Recent Angel decks have expanded on this concept, and many have an affirmation in addition to, or in place of, the title. *You are not alone* and *Your guardian angel watches over you* are two examples of 'titles' found on some of these cards. As you can imagine, drawing one of these can be a comforting experience. However, should you wish to pull any relevant details about your current situation, or guidance regarding your future path, these cards will likely be lacking. This is a good example of when a tool is set out for one job and cannot be easily shoe-horned into another: inspiration decks are not designed for divination and so struggle to fulfill this purpose. Deciding how your oracle will be used, and gearing it towards that, can prevent it from giving vague and clumsy answers later on.

Here are some common uses for oracles and how decks have been designed to cater to the reader...

Divination
These decks cover a broad scope of everyday life and spirituality to provide nuanced predictions.

Self Reflection
To facilitate the reader's self-exploration, these decks provide insights on emotions and inner life.

Inspiration
Often used for daily readings, these cards offer quotes and uplifting comments.

Healing
Shying away from darker, more challenging cards, these decks are geared towards the reader's emotional wellbeing.

Spiritual Practice
Delving into various spiritualities, these decks (such as astrological decks) are perfect for the more esoteric reader.

THINKING ABOUT ORACLE DECKS

It's often best to create the kind of deck that you yourself would get for personal use. These questions will help you explore how you use oracle decks so you can think about the kind you would like to create.

Why do you reach for an oracle deck?

....

....

....

....

....

....

....

What do you usually ask questions about?

....

....

....

....

....

....

....

Do you do complex spreads or daily card pulls?

....

....

....

....

....

....

What is missing from the options already available that you would like to see in a deck of cards?

....
....
....
....
....
....
....

How well do you think the cards fit your queries?

....
....
....
....
....
....
....

Do you prefer theme decks or ones that broadly apply to any area of life?

....
....
....
....
....
....
....

What can you bring to an oracle that would make it original?

....
....
....
....
....
....
....

Is there a particular mythology, story, or pop culture reference that would provide a new way of looking at traditional cards or inspire fresh thought?

....
....
....
....
....
....
....

DO YOU NEED A THEME?

If you are considering selling your deck or seeking publication, then a theme is often what will draw people to you. In the process of marketing, a theme can become a necessary hook, and it can broaden your deck's appeal. A tarot deck based on antique tattoos, for example, will attract more than just those with an interest in tarot card reading: tattoo enthusiasts will likely want to own a copy as well.

Themes can be exciting. They enable the creator to twist traditional symbols in fun and creative ways — and this can also affect the structure of the deck. In a witchcraft-themed tarot deck, a designer might want to adjust the suits of Wands, Cups, Swords, and Pentacles to Brooms, Cauldrons, Athames, and Pentagrams respectively, for example. The court cards or character cards (cards associated with different character types and people) are another element of the tarot that can be altered to suit a theme. In the *Mystical Cats Tarot* (by Lunaea Weatherstone and Mickie Mueller), Pages and Knights have adopted the more apt titles of Kittens and Toms.

Oracle decks are most often themed in terms of style, if not by subject. *The Vintage Wisdom Oracle Cards* by Victoria Moseley imposes its theme on the images rather than the titles. Crafted with antique postcards, the artist collaged vintage images together to create a deck that looks as though it has come from a bygone age. The titles and the card meanings, however, are not specifically vintage but rather timeless, and therefore broad enough to reflect modern readers' sensibilities, e.g.: *Awakening, Truth, Choice.*

EXERCISE

MOOD BOARD

It can be helpful to build a mood board for your theme! Pick a theme that appeals to you, e.g.: steampunk, fairy tales, urban life, vampires, LGBTQ+.

Then, consider these questions:

1. Does your theme have a specific historical context?
2. Where is your theme set in terms of geography (e.g.: the forest)?
3. Are there any particular characters that populate this theme? (e.g.: gods or monsters)

With these questions in mind, you can start building a mood board. You can do this on paper, cutting out images from magazines and books, or you can do this online via a site like Pinterest. Don't worry about being exact just yet — this exercise is just to give you a feel for your theme so that you'll have a collection of images to refer back to later!

Try it here :

WHAT ARE THE BASIC COMPONENTS OF AN ORACLE CARD?

The answer to this question is dependent on the needs of the user, since we all have different requirements. However, many of the following components are necessary to make your meaning immediately understandable to the reader.

MEANING

Before we get to the physical attributes of the card, let's think about the meaning. Each card in your deck should have a meaning attached. This is an exploration of your deck's theme: it fulfills your goals for the deck. Meanings for oracle cards can be vast and nuanced, so don't worry about tying it down yet — the more connotations a meaning has, the more flexible it will be for readings.

Once you've set your theme, think about how you can break it down into concepts. This can also become steps on a journey, different archetypes or events that could occur in someone's life. In the booklet that accompanies the deck, you can expand on the meaning of the card, delving into specifics or offering prompts for interpretation.

IMAGE

You might think that this is an obvious component to a card, but not necessarily so. There have been many successful decks that are text-based or which lack conventional images. However, for the majority of readers, an image is probably one of the most important parts of a card. It is often the images that first catch a potential reader's eye, so they can really make or break a deck.

Image styles vary wildly across oracle decks, from the brushes of the great masters to the vectors of digital designers — and a deck's success is greatly dependent on the tastes of the creator. But most of all, it is crucial that the picture conveys the card's meaning. For example, should a creator wish to design a card associated with abundance and happiness, it would make little sense to use a heavy and brooding palette, or include imagery of distant, dark clouds.

A good image should evoke a certain feeling in the reader. Its aim is to convey meaning and give rise to new understanding. A well-thought-out illustration can often bypass the other information on the face of a card.

TITLE

A title is usually printed at the top or bottom on the face of a card, though this is not always the case — some designers prefer to incorporate the title within the image or place it creatively in different positions. A title should be evocative of the meaning of the card; it can also be descriptive of the image. If the image is of an elephant, then you might expect to see that reflected in the card's title, however, some creators might use a word that describes the animal's attributes or mythology instead. Rather than Elephant, they might use something such as Memory for their title, since we are often told that elephants never forget.

The image and title are reflections of what the card represents. How you use them to convey this will contextualize it in the reader's mind. The title should act as a gateway into the image, shedding light on the card's primary meaning. The title is also useful if a guidebook is included with the cards; being able to locate a meaning in a book can be a chore if there is nothing written on the card to help identify it.

That being said, not all cards have titles. Some readers prefer not to be restricted by a designer's intention and will wish to create their own bond with the set of images. Both editions of The SoulCards by Deborah Koff-Chapin contain 60 cards apiece. None of the 120 cards have titles on them and there are no definitions within the book that comes as part of each deck. This allows the reader to develop their own intuitive link with the paintings. Any symbolism within the images is subjective, and interpretation is solely reliant upon the person viewing the cards.

KEYWORDS

People either love them or hate them, but keywords (additional words to aid description) have become a popular feature of the oracle deck. A keyword can be extremely useful. Using the example of the Elephant once again, its name can only reveal so much. While the card could draw on the idea of an elephant never forgetting, the animal might also represent being large or fiercely protective. If a keyword or two is added beneath the title, it can shed more light on the meaning of each card.

But what if the reader's idea of the animal is different to your own? For some, having these extra keywords for the Elephant will be helpful, reminding them of what they've already learned from the guidebook. For others, some keywords might conflict with their understanding of the symbol. Deciding on whether keywords will be a help or hindrance is up to the creator, but it could be of benefit to do a little market research beforehand. Once again, adding keywords to a deck can make or break a purchase — and if the deck is for personal use, they could present a lifeline in a difficult reading.

NUMBERING

Numbering is sometimes used to identify cards. Practically speaking, numbers are a quick and easy way to find the card's meaning in a guidebook, which is why many publishers place them on the card faces. Some oracles will be split into different sections (sometimes called suits) and numbers, along with titles, are ways of identifying those different groups.

But it's not just about practicality: numbering the cards is a good way to start thinking about how each card in your deck interacts with the others. Are there any concepts that feel like they should be at the beginning, middle, or end of the deck order? And do numbers match any of the themes? In some cases, a number will have numerological significance — for instance, the number two is most commonly associated with partnerships, choices and opposites.

BACK DESIGN

Some card decks are double-sided. The Vice-Versa Tarot is a good example of one such: with 78 traditional tarot images on the front of the cards, each has a different perspective of the scene printed on its reverse. However, this is a rarity, and most tarot and oracle decks will have a uniform design on their backs.

Although it is the front of the card that we spend most of our time looking at, you'd be surprised by how desirable some decks have become because of their back design. Most readers will lay cards out face down, so it is important for the backs to be attractive and in keeping with the style of the deck as a whole.

In terms of tarot, having a reversible back design (which looks the same upside down as it does right side up) is necessary for those who use reversals. A reversal is a slightly different interpretation of a card, and many readers shuffle the deck so that some cards are randomly reversed. A reader will not want to know whether cards are upright or reversed when shuffling, so a reversible image on the backs will mean that they're none the wiser until the cards are turned.

As you may have gathered, a designer can use one or all of the above components when creating an oracle. While not every component is entirely necessary for a variety of decks, if you're creating your own version of the tarot, Lenormand, or Kipper decks, it's a good idea to use the traditional titles in order to keep it recognizable.

Page Left: Photography by Bright, S. Card from *The Luna Sol Tarot*, Medaglia, K. and Shill, D.

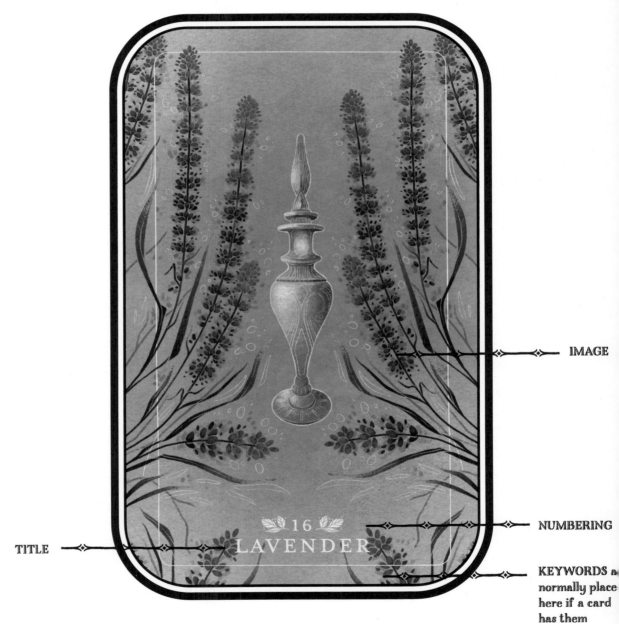

IMAGE

NUMBERING

TITLE

KEYWORDS a normally place here if a card has them

Try designing a card here :

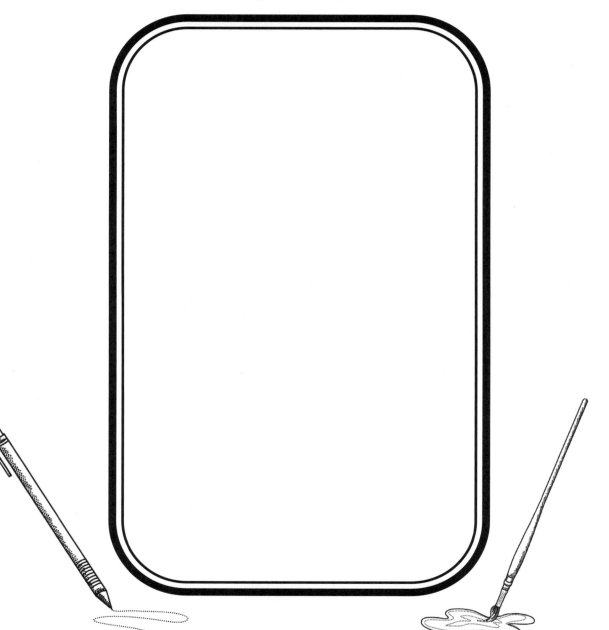

HOW MANY ORACLE CARDS DO YOU NEED?

How many cards are used within an oracle is really down to personal preference. The following thoughts should be considered, though:

- A deck will need to be robust enough to answer a variety of questions in a multitude of different ways, so having a diverse range of cards is important. 20 cards might not be enough to effectively acknowledge all of life's trials, tribulations and joys. The more cards, the more possibilities you will have at your disposal!

- The more cards in a deck, the more cumbersome it can be to work with. Keep your deck concise. If it starts getting too long (tarot's 78 cards are probably the maximum), ask yourself: What meanings are essential to the deck and which are superfluous?

- Keep in mind that some cards can work in combination to create more meanings. Even if you have fewer cards in your deck, that doesn't mean that there are fewer interpretations available!

- Too few cards can be frustrating. If a deck is used regularly, then a smaller number will result in certain cards turning up frequently. Although this might be helpful in some readings, repeating cards could also become an annoyance.

- The number of cards in your deck should be dictated by the meanings themselves. Remember that you're telling a story. Plan what you want to convey, then break this down into individual meanings. How long or short the deck is should be determined in this part of the planning process.

- Don't forget nuance! After all, there are many ways to describe both happiness and sadness. Finding ways to do this in the planning process will help to fine-tune your oracle and give a fuller reading experience.

STRUCTURES AND SYSTEMS

One of the differences between most oracles and a system-based card deck such as the tarot is that an oracle deck can have as many or as few cards as one wishes. There really is no set formula, though it has become popular in recent times for Angel decks to consist of 44 cards (which relates to the triplicate 444, the 'angel number' thought to signify celestial love and support). Generally, though, there is no recommended quantity of cards: some oracles will contain up to 100 cards, whereas some have as few as 20.

TAROT	ORACLES
78 cards in total	No set system or structure
Split into two sections: the Major and Minor Arcana	Often theme based
Major Arcana has 22 numbered cards, also known as trumps	Cards expand on and explore the theme, e.g.: angels, fairies, mermaids
Minor Arcana is based on classic card suits and is divided into four groups of 16	Oracle creators draw from many different influences
Each card has a detailed esoteric meaning conveyed by symbols within the art	Because decks are thematic, there are fewer correspondances than with tarot — you're more likely to get an entire deck dedicated to astrology rather than find astrological correspondences within a deck following a different theme
Major Arcana concerns big life events and charts an individual's spiritual evolution.	Each card in an oracle has a clear topic as opposed to the many hidden nuances of tarot cards
Minor Arcana deals with practical concerns and the magic that can be found in the everyday.	An oracle has as many or as few cards as the creator wishes
Tarot cards include correspondances to elements, alchemy, astrology, mythology, Kabbalah, and other spiritual systems	

ACE of CUPS

THE WORLD

THE HANGED ONE

KING of WANDS

Due to the lack of rules involved in creating an oracle, a system is not necessary, but some creators find that incorporating a system can provide structure. For example, the *Angels and Ancestors Oracle* by Kyle Gray is a 55-card deck split into four parts. The bulk of the cards are dedicated to 30 'Sacred Ones': the medicine people, shamans, and warriors, for instance, who share their experience and insight with the user. The next section includes 12 spirits that come under the heading of 'Guardians and Messengers'. The final cards are split into two further groups: 'Warrior Symbols' (such as *Drum, Broken Arrow and Sun*), and four 'Seasons' cards.

In this way, Kyle Gray extrapolated a structure from his theme, segmenting the deck into groups of character cards ('Sacred Ones' and 'Guardians and Messengers'), symbols, and seasons. Once you have set a theme for your deck, think about the different ways in which this can be applied to your structure…

Above and Below: *The Luna Sol Tarot,* Medaglia, K. and Shill, D.

QUEEN of DISKS

FIVE of SWORDS

PAGE of WANDS

THE MOON

EXERCISE

CREATING A STRUCTURE

1. What is your theme?
2. Are there any clear groupings that arise out of your theme? E.g.: a mythology-themed deck could be grouped into Gods, Heroes, Monsters, etc.
3. How do these groups relate to each other?
4. Are there any existing magical or spiritual systems that you want to evoke? Can they provide structure?

Structure can provide extra weight in a reading. For example, if a deck is broken up into the elements then the drawing of a card connected to water might hint at there being an emotional link to the overall issue, since water is often associated with feelings. Should more than one card from this group appear or 'dominate', then the reading is either tapping into an emotional situation or suggesting that the reader assess how they are dealing with their emotions.

1.

....

....

2.

....

....

....

3.

....

....

....

....

....

4.

....

....

....

Page Right: Photography by Bright, S. Card from *The Seed and Sickle Oracle Deck*. Inkwright, F.

two of torches

Queen of Swords

King of Cups

Princess of Pentacles

Prince of Wands

two of cups

CHARACTER CARDS

Not all oracle decks contain characters, and this can sometimes prevent them from describing the very people we might wish to ask the cards about. The tarot system has a well-thought-out selection of 16 character cards (generally referred to as court cards). Separated by age, hierarchy, and personality traits relating to their element, each court card can help us to loosely identify people we know within our readings. As an example, the *Page of Wands* (the suit associated with fire) is representative of a young, enthusiastic, and creative person, whereas the *Queen of Swords* (air) describes a mature person with feminine energy, respected for their honesty and no-nonsense approach to life.

Within both the Lenormand and Kipper systems, you will find a *Man* and *Woman* card, as well as a *Child* and *Rider*. These character cards are important because they denote people within readings, rather than events or consequences of actions. It's worth thinking about whether you want to include character cards in your deck, since they add something to a reading that isn't otherwise present. You don't have to be tied down to gender — some decks prefer to use archetypes, and some Lenormand creators, like James R. Eads, have even added the neutral *Person* to their decks to be more inclusive.

Of course, character cards don't necessarily have to refer to people. For example, some of the symbolic meanings for the *Child* card within the Lenormand system are 'new beginnings' and 'something small or the reduction of something'. Before you start, decide whether you want your character cards to refer specifically to people in the reader's life or whether they can have allegorical meanings as well. This will affect how you create the cards and set their meanings.

Not every character card will be as obvious as those mentioned above. The following examples suggest ways of bringing character into your deck in a more general manner.

Page Left: *The Cosmic Slumber Tarot*, Walden, T.

BOSS

If you want your oracle deck to cater to readings about career and work, the *Boss* card makes sense. This card would suggest someone superior to the reader, someone who has some control or authority over them. The meaning, when in readings connected to other areas of life, might concern someone who is overbearing and controlling: a pushy friend or dominant lover could be suggested when this card is in play.

ENEMY

CHILD

The *Child* represents young people. If you want your character cards to have allegorical meanings, this card could relate to someone who is young at heart, naive, childish, or perhaps someone who is playing the role of the child in a certain situation (e.g.: someone who has just moved to a new country). If you would rather that your *Child* card only represent people under a certain age, think about how you can make that clear in the artwork or accompanying booklet of meanings.

It's always useful to know when someone is opposed to you, and this card can highlight a detractor or rival in your readings. The title possibly sounds more dramatic than it actually is — appearing more in line with the villains of fiction — but it does, nonetheless, alert a reader to an opponent: someone who does not have their best interests at heart.

FRIEND

A friend is someone with whom you have a mutual bond of affection. This could be someone you share interests with, but the most common meaning for a card like this is someone who has your back, is trustworthy and is willing to listen to you when you're at your worst as well as your best. While some people consider family members and lovers to be amongst their best friends, within the oracular system this can blur the lines. It is important to remember that this card speaks directly about those not connected to you through blood, marriage or romance.

FAMILY MEMBER

The *Family Member* card refers to anyone you are linked to by blood or marriage. This includes parents, siblings, cousins, aunts, uncles, grandparents, children, in-laws, or stepfamily. Someone who 'feels like a sister to me' is not depicted by this card and would fall under the umbrella of *Friend*.

LOVER

A lover is considered to be someone you are involved with in a sexual or loving relationship. In some cases, it will concern an ex-lover, depending on the cards that surround it. The Lenormand system especially uses this methodology: the cards are understood in relation to cards drawn next to them. On its own, this card means a present lover, but if drawn with a card representing the past then it would mean an ex-lover. Similarly, if the card placed next to the Lover is suggestive of new beginnings, that would point in the direction of a fresh courtship — while a card concerning deception could suggest an affair.

There will always be cards that unsettle a reader and the *Thief* is one of them. However, if we wish for our oracle deck to reflect life and provide warnings, then it is vital that we allow it to do so without censoring those parts of our day-to-day lives that leave us feeling uncomfortable or fearful. If there is a thief in your midst, would you not rather know?

The *Thief* card describes someone who takes from us. Most of us will think of a robber, someone intent on stealing our money or personal possessions. While this card could be describing physical theft, there are other suggestions worth considering when the card is drawn. It could act as a reminder to check all forms of security. Has someone in the workplace stolen your idea or has your art been copied? Or perhaps it's more abstract: Have you become a victim of an energy vampire? Is someone draining you of your vitality as a way of refueling their own?

This card could represent a policeman, for example, or anyone with an official title or badge of authority. A judge (especially if paired with cards relating to justice), a member of parliament or a member of the religious clergy may also be described when the *Officiant* card is drawn.

The *Colleague* is, quite literally, anyone with whom you work. If you work within a team environment, then chances are this card will be pointing at someone amongst them. If you work alone, then it will refer to anyone who might assist you, from suppliers to postal workers or even your competitors. When joined with a card associated with love, you may find affection, romance or even a sexual encounter within the world of work. If partnered with cards representing an ending, it might predict a project or job coming to an end.

COLLEAGUE

WISE ELDER

A wise elder can represent anyone who has experience and wisdom on their side. The people described by this card tend to be mature in years — maybe a grandparent, elderly neighbor or a mentor — but while the age of the person is a telltale sign when working out who it might signify, the true emphasis is on the wisdom they impart.

The *Stranger* card is an interesting one because it describes someone we have not yet been personally acquainted with. A stranger might manifest as a new partner, buyer for your home, employer or reliable employee. The cards around it should help to decipher who this person is or why they are entering your story. In some instances, when a negative card is drawn alongside it, the *Stranger* might come as a warning. It is unlikely that they will turn out to be a masked murderer or violent intruder, but could, for instance, represent a faceless troll or someone hiding behind their internet screen.

STRANGER

CHARACTER CARDS

Think about four character cards that you would like to place in your deck and explore
what these characters might mean, e.g.:

Character	Thief
Attributes	Wily, cunning, resourceful, deceptive, greedy
Themes	Defiance of society, crime, moral ambiguity, loss
Allegorical Meaning	A person, or a situation, that has robbed the reader of something dear to them

Character	
Attributes	
Themes	
Allegorical Meaning	

Character	
Attributes	
Themes	
Allegorical Meaning	

Character	
Attributes	
Themes	
Allegorical Meaning	

SECTIONS AND SUITS

Structuring your deck into clear, separate sections can make it more versatile for readings. Some readers like to separate the sections when doing a reading so they can get specific answers for their topic. To use Kyle Gray's deck as an example, the group of seasonal cards would be apt for answering a question about timing, while the symbols of the warrior may work for advice about a method of action or skill that is needed for moving forward.

The following spread shows how the traditional tarot deck can be used in the same way for a romantic reading. Drawing a card from each of the following groups, insight will be gained about a person's next potential relationship.

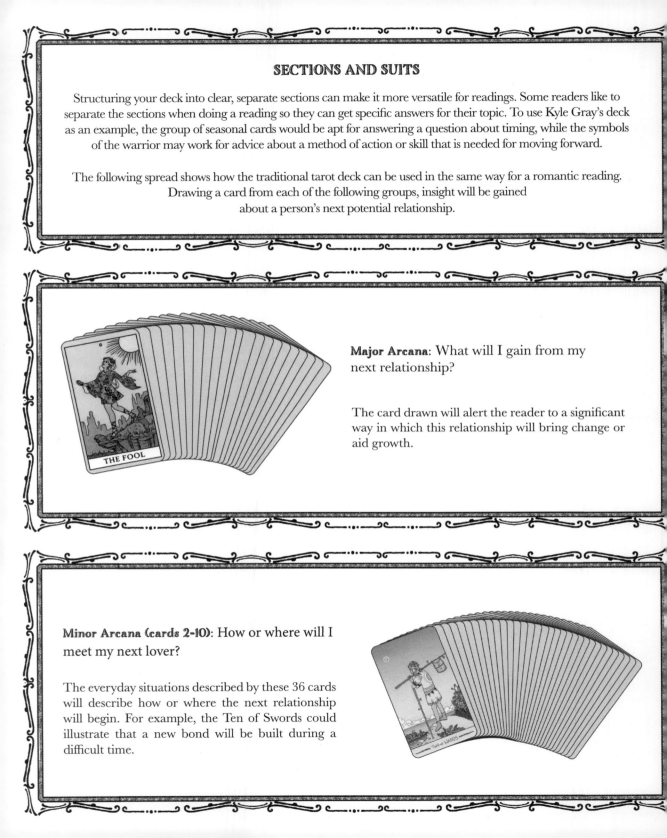

Major Arcana: What will I gain from my next relationship?

The card drawn will alert the reader to a significant way in which this relationship will bring change or aid growth.

Minor Arcana (cards 2–10): How or where will I meet my next lover?

The everyday situations described by these 36 cards will describe how or where the next relationship will begin. For example, the Ten of Swords could illustrate that a new bond will be built during a difficult time.

Court Cards: How will I recognize my next potential partner?

These 16 cards will highlight a dominant personality trait of your next lover.

· QUEEN OF PENTACLES ·

Aces: When will this person come into my life?

Depending on your own seasonal associations, one of the four Aces will alert you to a season in the year.

ACE OF CUPS

Page Left:
Modern Witch Tarot, Sterle, L.
The Luna Sol Tarot, Medaglia, K. and Shill, D.
Page Right:
Mystical Medleys: A Vintage Cartoon Tarot, Hall, G.
White Numen: A Sacred Animal Tarot. Gonzalez, A.

But how do you create sections within your deck? The concept of time can help to impose a structure on your deck and will also add depth to readings. Oracle creators like Kyle Gray and James R. Eads use seasons as sections for their decks. You could go one step further and incorporate equinox festivals, Wiccan sabbats, or other spiritual calendar events as a way of introducing structure to your deck.

But it's not just structure that this helps with — the timing of the readings themselves can also add depth. A morning or evening setting for a card may alter its meaning dramatically. Something as simple as adding bright sunshine or snow to a card can be indicative of a specific time period in the year. Within tarot, an ace brimming with new activity could symbolize spring, whereas one brushed with the discarded leaves of autumn will hint at events taking place towards the later part of the year.

The age of character cards can also be suggestive of either starting out or winding down from a journey. Children are representative of new beginnings and growth, whereas the elderly might suggest something coming to an end.

Surrounding: *The Seed and Sickle Oracle Deck*, Inkwright, F.

HOW TO CREATE SECTIONS IN AN ORACLE DECK...

Characters
A series of characters separates this section from the rest of the deck.

Seasons
Seasons are suggestive of timing and can provide the framework behind the suits.

Elements
Elements can refer to different areas of life and are associated with certain themes (air, for example, is associated with the mind, thoughts and communication). These themes can provide a basis for the cards in these suits.

Spiritual Systems
Spiritualities can provide a basis for structure: the 12 signs of the Zodiac, the seven chakras or Archangels are often used as standalone sections in an oracle deck.

Stories
Some decks have well-known stories running through them (like the Mythic Tarot by Juliet Sharman-Burke and Liz Greene) — and folklore often provides its own structure.

When a deck is not divided into sections, we are basically suggesting that every card in the deck is equal in value. Though most oracles work on this premise, there is still often an underlying structure, even if the deck isn't clearly segmented into sections. Even the simple balance of positive and negative, or uplifting and challenging cards, is consciously created by the designer, ensuring that there's an even split in the deck to make for fair readings.

Before you begin, think about how a system or sense of structure can aid or hinder your oracle. While some readers will just pull a card in the morning for inspiration, others have dynamic, intricate questions to ask — and therefore require a full cast, narrative, challenge, and dialogue within their readings.

HOW WILL YOUR CARDS AFFECT ONE ANOTHER?

Thinking about how your cards will work together and whether they will interact within readings is another consideration to get your head around before you start. There are some cards that prefer to stand by themselves, whereas others depend on groupings and association.

The Lenormand, as an obvious example, is traditionally read in multiples. Each card acts like a word in a sentence and does not stand by itself comfortably. The symbol of the tree, when read in a Lenormand deck, can speak of health — but without a card to accompany it, the context of the message is missing. We would need another card to flesh out the symbol's meaning. When beside *The Clover*, for instance, a boost to someone's wellbeing is likely since this is a card of luck. If the darker side of *The Clouds* edged up beside *The Tree*, we would therefore determine that someone might be facing general health problems; with *The Gentleman* or *The Lady* card, maybe a doctor is foreseen.

Cards such as these will allow your intuition to soar since there are endless combinations and interpretations that can arise from different duos and trios. However, it is the matter-of-fact nature and directness of their delivery that makes them successful in predictions of things to come. When creating cards that work in combination, really consider the symbols and how they will partner up before you get down to designing the actual cards. What would the symbol of a train mean when united with a house? Could it suggest a visit to see someone far away, or even that your own relocation is on the horizon?

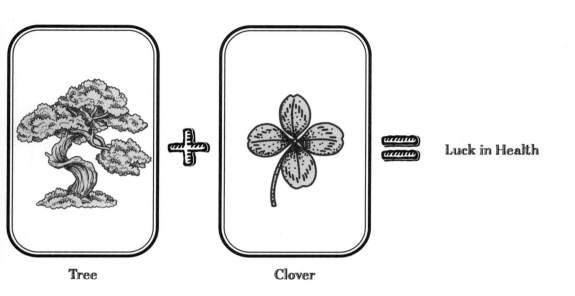

Tree + Clover = Luck in Health

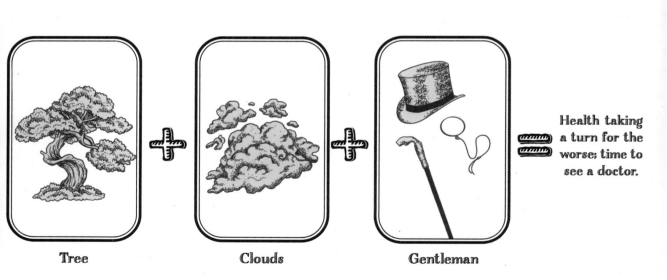

Tree + Clouds + Gentleman = Health taking a turn for the worse; time to see a doctor.

The less-understood Kipper cards are similar to the Lenormand (in that the cards work in combination) but vary in many other ways. While they do not contain symbolic imagery or religious symbols, they are read in clusters and are dependent on direction — the way in which a specific card's character is pointing, and who or what they are pointing at, is vital to interpretation. As an example, in the traditional Bavarian method, we would hope that the *Man* and *Woman* cards face one another in a reading. If, by a twist of fate, they end up drawn back-to-back, or sit far away from each other in a spread, we can determine that there are difficulties between the person being read for and the person relating to their question.

Many of today's modern oracles are less inclined to affect each other in this way. The cards from the more affirmation-based oracles have their own individual agendas and are less easily mixed: each is intended to pack a punch on its own. While they may be read as a collective in spreads, they are less likely to interact in the same way as the Lenormand cards or directionally like the Kipper. Considering direction in your cards can make for some interesting scenarios in a reading — and again, this creates a system for your deck.

APUS

ORION

PERSEUS

72

TAURUS

Page Left: *White Numen: A Sacred Animal Tarot - Special Limited Edition, Golden Constellation Oracle Deck, Gonzalez, A.*

THE PILGRIM

THE CHAMPION

THE POET

THE HOUND

THE WALKER

Page Right: *The Seed and Sickle Oracle Deck - Special Limited Edition, The Citadel Deck, Inkwright, F.*

CREATING A NARRATIVE

THE WISE ONE

Let's say, for argument's sake, that we want to keep your oracle relatively general. This would mean that a whole range of scenarios and sub-plots will need to exist within the cards, making it flexible and accessible to a wide range of questions. While the cards will need to be specific in their intention, they must be abstract enough to cover more than one area of interest. Anyone who has asked a question of the cards about love and received a response more suited to a business reading will sympathize with this.

You can still create a narrative within your deck, however. This will give a sense of progression and will really help the reader check in with themselves. The tarot's Major Arcana is perhaps the best example of how a narrative helps readings. The 22 cards are all steps on a spiritual journey to self-actualization and enlightenment. These steps are not all easy — *The Wheel of Fortune* can herald unexpected changes, The Tower is notorious for what you've built crumbling before you, and Death signifies the end of a life chapter. But others are uplifting (*The Sun*) or introspective (*The Hermit*), heralding big life events or inviting you to turn your attention in a certain direction. Because each card is a step on a journey, the Majors allow you to keep track of whatever path you're on when they appear in readings — and if you keep a record, you can refer back to previous readings to find any pattern that starts to build between them.

So, when you're planning your oracle, think of what narrative you want to create and how that will affect the readings. If you have a clear theme, this can inform your narrative. Folklore and mythology often have narrative patterns; could your deck's narrative follow the stages of the archetypal Hero's Journey, for instance?

Page Right: *The Seed and Sickle Oracle Deck · Special Limited Edition, The Citadel Deck*, Inkwright, F.

CARD MEANINGS

It can be tempting to put a selection of images together and give each a title without considering how they will be used. This will, indeed, give you an oracle but how well will it work? For a truly versatile and nuanced deck, you need to know what each card means.

This is when all the elements we've gone over so far come into play. Your card meanings should tell a story. They should be grouped into whatever sections you've chosen to structure your deck with, they should give enough breadth of scope that they can be used for a diverse divination reading, they should communicate your theme and your goal, and they will provide the template for whatever design you choose to put on your card, whether you're creating the artwork from scratch or using pre-existing artwork (as we'll explore in the next chapter).

The heart of your card is its meaning: it's what you want to say to the reader. Many oracle creators use broad concepts as a basis for their card meanings, like *Balance, Truth*, or *Conflict*. The tarot is more esoteric, with concepts like *Temperance*, and incorporates character archetypes (as we saw in the Character Cards section). If you have a specific theme, you may want to tailor your meanings to that; for an urban deck, for instance, you could feature card meanings such as *Transit, Community*, and *Business*. Of course, the meaning goes far beyond the title itself. The potential meanings of a card are vast. While you can be very pragmatic in your approach and rooted in one idea (like the Lenormand), a more esoteric approach (like that of the tarot) can open up your deck to infinite interpretations. Don't be afraid to pack meaning into your cards: just remain focused on the title and you'll be able to use just one card to unlock a whole world within the reader! If you want to publish your deck, you'll be able to express the details of your card meanings in an accompanying booklet (see the chapter Companion Books).

AN ORACLE SAMPLE

What follows are 15 examples of card meanings along with reasons for why each card might be included. These track the deck's narrative, which is that of a life's journey — everything from humble or exciting beginnings to fulfilled or regretful endings, charting success to misfortune or hardship to abundance. These meanings give an oracle form and reference topics that most people will be able to relate to or have already experienced on their lifepath. At the end of each description, a short list of possible symbols or visual metaphors are listed to inspire the creator — something we'll go over in greater depth in the next chapter (Designing Your Oracle).

As well as providing examples, hopefully these cards will spark some ideas. These concepts are prevalent across many oracle decks, so you can use them as a jumping-off point to expand on them or make them more specific to your own theme.

ADVENTURE:

An adventure can mean different things to different people. Most likely, on a mundane level, the card will describe a new job, a commitment to a new relationship or even a vacation. Operating as a doorway to exciting times ahead, this card can be inspirational for the person drawing it. Although *Adventure* can be predictive, its job within the oracle is to spur someone on and encourage action.

VISUAL LINKS

a hiking trip, a map, a compass, a ship, packed bags or a suitcase

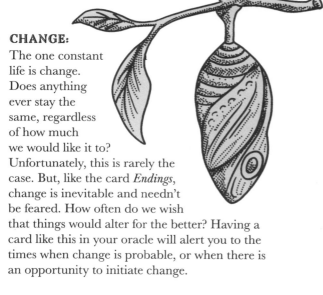

CHANGE:

The one constant life is change. Does anything ever stay the same, regardless of how much we would like it to? Unfortunately, this is rarely the case. But, like the card *Endings*, change is inevitable and needn't be feared. How often do we wish that things would alter for the better? Having a card like this in your oracle will alert you to the times when change is probable, or when there is an opportunity to initiate change.

Change is a neutral card within the deck, unless you choose to flesh it out by preceding the word with *positive* or *negative*. In itself, it doesn't really say much more than that: like other cards, its meaning is defined by the cards that accompany it or by the meaning that the reader has ascribed to its placement within a spread.

VISUAL LINKS

a turning wheel, the four seasons, a road sign suggesting a diversion, a caterpillar and butterfly.

BALANCE:

In a reading, this card will detect a need for balancing out aspects of your own life. Are you overworked, overemotional, or burning the candle at both ends? Sometimes, it may be relevant to look at the cards on either side to see if they offer any clues as to what is out of balance, or to draw another to see what is uneven. A card such as *Home* might indicate that are you spending too much time in your comfort zone, for example.

VISUAL LINKS

a set of scales, balancing on a wire, a yoga pose that requires balance, a yin and yang symbol, the mixing of opposing substances.

CHOICE:

Choice is an important part of the oracle because it calls a person to action. Whereas some cards can offer comfort, this card requires the person being read for to do something. In a reading, it is imperative that some cards encourage the seeker to consider options and provoke them to administer real change. We must remember that the real work begins when a person has left the reading table.

This card is suggestive of two paths — you either choose one or the other. In a reading geared towards love, it could highlight the need to choose between two prospective partners, or a desire to stay or leave an existing relationship. In a career-based reading, two different jobs might be on offer, or you may be called to think about the different ways in which you respond to a problem.

VISUAL LINKS

two doors, different pathways, a fork in the road, an angel and a devil seated on opposite shoulders

CONFLICT:

One of the benefits of an oracle is that a reader can sometimes detect a situation in the cards before it arises and get one step ahead of it. When a card such as *Conflict* shows up, depending on where it is placed, an upcoming dispute could be avoided or defused. At worst, the heads-up from the oracle will allow you to be

prepared. There will be scenarios in which conflict is inevitable and impossible to avoid, but, in a positive sense, the card can describe those times when standing up for yourself against opposition is imperative. Therefore, this is a much-needed card within the oracle if we are intending to encompass a well-rounded version of life.

It's also important to pick out nuanced ideas within your deck. If you have the card *Conflict* but intend for it to refer to friendly rivalries, then perhaps you should add the card *Competition* to let this idea stand on its own.

VISUAL LINKS

boxing gloves, a tug of war, two people head-to-head or back-to-back.

ENDINGS:

We experience endings all the time but this does not always need to be as negative as it sounds. Tarot's *Death* card is the most famous when it comes to delivering last rites, but due to its visual symbolism (that of the reaper and scythe), it has evolved into an omen that is feared rather than one to be welcomed or celebrated. Endings are simply a fact of life. In order for us to mature, we must say goodbye to our youth. Similarly, our innocence is replaced by wisdom. Not every ending is bad, even if the transition it brings is a difficult one to pass through.

VISUAL LINKS

a reaper, a gravestone, a scythe, a skull, a burned-out candle, a bone.

HOME:

The *Home* card can be interpreted in more than one way. As an actual place of residence, it can speak of the physical structure that you live in. However, the card has more symbolic references when in an oracle. If we think about the saying 'home is where the heart is', its link to personal and emotional security is obvious.

The *Home* card can refer to the stability and wellbeing of the person being read for. This is one of a handful of neutral cards in a deck; it really needs something else to bounce off to define its meaning. If the card is highlighting the security of the seeker and is joined by *Conflict*, as an example, it suggests that comfort is being challenged. If *Focus* partners up with *Home*, then it advises that a person's stability (be it physical, mental, or emotional) is in question and could need extra care and attention.

VISUAL LINKS
a house, a houseboat, a nest, a bird house.

LOVE:

Love is an essential card for many readers. Of course, it can alert us to romance and romantic possibility within a reading, but it is so much more than just that — and here is where you start to see how your card's meaning, although apparently oblique, could contain many nuances that will only expand the possibilities for interpretation.

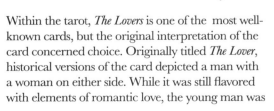

Within the tarot, *The Lovers* is one of the most well-known cards, but the original interpretation of the card concerned choice. Originally titled *The Lover*, historical versions of the card depicted a man with a woman on either side. While it was still flavored with elements of romantic love, the young man was

required to make a choice between one or the other. In modern tarots that follow the *Rider-Waite-Smith* system, the third figure is some kind of celestial creature which symbolizes higher knowledge that can be attained through romantic love, or via the union between the self and the other. Here we can see a clear distinction between the two systems — but in both instances, the meaning of the card is much deeper than just that of romantic love.

If you want to include a *Love* card that really explores this concept, don't fall into the trap of thinking that this card only predicts a new boyfriend or girlfriend coming into the seeker's life. The love of a job, or even a need for self-acceptance and self-care could be equally as important. Love is often what drives us, so how can you explore that in your card meaning?

VISUAL LINKS
a red heart, a couple, friends, parent and child, a kiss or embrace, a red rose.

MISFORTUNE:

Not all misfortunes will be life changing. Whereas the card can certainly describe those times when we are down on our luck

and cannot see a way out — such as crippling debt, illness, or the falling-through of a house sale — it can also pinpoint those days when we miss out on something which, while less significant, can also cause frustration. As with all card readings, the key to interpretation is often in the context of the question. If *Misfortune* falls into a yearly reading, it is more likely to imply a greater impact than if describing the events of an afternoon. On the whole, the extent of the bad luck suggested will depend on the parameters you have assigned to the reading.

VISUAL LINKS
broken vase, smashed window, a dark cloud, exploding volcano, cracked mirror

OBSTACLES:

Life can be a little bit like a game of Monopoly: one moment, you're breezing around the board, banking all of the money but suddenly, by chance, you fall on a space belonging to an opponent and end up having to part with a bucketload of cash. In order for your oracle to be realistic, there need to be cards that address obstacles and setbacks.

An obstacle can have many faces. Other cards will help to determine what is causing the obstruction, be it authority, love, unexpected changes or something more literal, such as a problem connected with the home or money. Obstacles need not be insurmountable, though. In fact, in some situations, it is the bumps in the road that help us to grow and learn. Can you think back to a time when a difficulty, conflict or rejection actually set you off on a better route or helped to make you grow stronger? In this sense, these hindrances could be described as blessings, since they sometimes encourage us to carve out a greater and more fulfilling path than we might previously have imagined.

VISUAL LINKS
roadblock, mountain, a fallen tree, a broken bridge, a hole in the road

OPPORTUNITY:

An opportunity is something that many clients look for in their readings. Those who are wanting a new soulmate seek indications of chance through favorable cards in the hope of meeting their Mr/Ms/Mx Right. If the deck is sprinkled with cards that can flesh out what to be on the lookout for — namely the *wheres, whens,* and *hows* — a reading can provide clues as to how the opportunity for love might manifest and where it may be found. The same is true for those seeking a job or a new direction in life.

Opportunity can help a seeker remain optimistic about their future. The potential indicated by this card rests on their own willpower and belief. In order for someone to take advantage of this, they must take action. A reading is most effective when a person uses

the information held within it to alter their life for the better. Receiving the card *Opportunity* puts power in the hands of the person being read for.

VISUAL LINKS
an open door, a gateway, a key and/or keyhole, a ladder.

PAST:

The *Past*, when in the oracle deck, can refer to our distant memories, but needn't go back that far. When it is turned over in a reading, this card can signify something of importance from the recent past too. In short, it can highlight something that needs revisiting or reconsidering but, when accompanied by the right card (be it one that indicates a person or a relationship), you may instead be about to face some kind of reunion. This card can bring back ex-lovers, old friends, or emotions that we thought we had already dealt with (or that we had swept under the carpet).

VISUAL LINKS
a clock, an old sepia photograph, a bygone era

POWER:

Power is an interesting quality to consider. When it turns up in a reading, we could take it to be an obvious sign of our own personal capability or influence. We might not always feel powerful but being so does not necessarily mean exercising force or dominance. Walking away from something, as an example, can be an extremely powerful way of affecting a relationship or situation. Keeping silent, as well as speaking up, can also influence the results of something or strengthen your position. Even if you are amongst many, your voice as part of the collective can become a force to be reckoned with.

When this card turns up in a reading, it suggests that you have access to power. However, as a card by itself, it does not describe how you use it. If the card sits with a character card or answers a question relating to a specific person or situation, then it might be important for you to consider what power this person could have over you or how you may exert your power over them.

VISUAL LINKS

a clenched fist, a lightning flash, a crown

SOLITUDE:

Not everyone enjoys being by themselves. For some, solitude can feel isolating and, should they be alone with their thoughts, boring or even scary. In a recent study made public by *Science Magazine*, many of the people asked said they'd rather give themselves a mild electric shock than be deprived of external stimuli.

Solitude does not need to be about loneliness though. Of course, there will be times when the card describes isolation or even abandonment — but, on a general level, Solitude can awaken us to the benefits of being by ourselves. There will always be occasions when we have to figure something out without others influencing our decision and this card will encourage a retreat of some kind.

VISUAL LINKS

alone on a desert island, a traditional hermit with lamp and staff, someone out in nature with no human contact, a hut in the forest.

PATIENCE:

Within the oracle, it is advantageous to have cards that offer guidance around timing. Discerning when something will happen can be difficult, so cards such as Patience are a useful addition to your deck. *Patience* indicates that something will take longer to manifest, and that it might test our ability to tolerate delays without becoming agitated. It is important to remember that some things are worth waiting for.

VISUAL LINKS

hourglass, moon cycles, pregnancy, a snail, a chair

EXERCISE

CREATING CARD MEANINGS

As a warm-up, pick a story that you love. Using the stages of the story, write 10 card meanings. E.g.: From the nursery rhyme *Jack and Jill*, we could get the card meanings of *Goal* (the pail of water), *Ascension* (going up the hill), *Tragedy* (Jack fell down), etc. As an extra step, write these meanings as titles on pieces of paper, then shuffle them and see if you can do a reading using just these cards!

No.	Card Meaning	Image/Idea
1		
2		
3		
4		
5		
6		
7		
8		
9		
10		

CHOOSING A TITLE

Choosing a title for your card deck must not be left as an afterthought. If you are selling your deck, then the title by which it is referred to is going to be extremely important and could make a big difference to whether someone buys your pack or not. Here are a few tips:

- *Be honest.* One marketing ploy for selling cards is to add words that might attract a buyer. I have lost count of how many oracle decks I have seen over the years that have used the word 'tarot' within their title — despite the fact that they do not follow the traditional tarot system. This is sometimes done to give the deck greater credibility, but, most often, it's done to appeal to the tarot reader. This is a bad business move since it is deceptive and misleading. Those looking to buy a tarot deck will expect all of the features of a traditional tarot and will shun anything that pretends to be something it is not. This is also true of a Lenormand and Kipper reader. Be honest about what is in the box. If your deck is an oracle, you would be foolish to state that it is anything other than that in your title.
- *Keep it concise.* While you may wish to give your deck an elaborate title, remember that it might easily be forgotten or mispronounced. The original title for my tarot deck, *Spirit Within Tarot*, was *Spirit Within the Shadows Tarot*. This is not an overly elaborate example, but the shorter version is certainly easier for people to remember. People will likely look for your deck in search engines and on YouTube and a long title will make this a chore — especially if they continue to type it incorrectly due to the title's intricacies. Remember that this title will also need to fit comfortably on your box or logos.
- *Make sure your title doesn't already exist.* There are, in existence, decks with the same title (check out both *The Witches Tarot* and *The Steampunk Tarot*). It's possible that your idea for a title has already been thought of and used. Before you begin to publicize your cards, it's worth doing a search and finding out if someone has already created a product with the same name. Not doing so could lead to conflict with other creators, potentially leading to legal issues regarding copyright.
- *Don't walk the well-worn path.* There are many words that have become overused. You will find many tarot and oracle decks with the word enchanted in their titles, for example. Do you want to add to these or come up with something that will not have readers confused by which deck is the recent topic of conversation?

DO YOUR CARDS WORK?

One of the real purposes of planning an oracle is to make sure that it actually works. I am sure that I am not the only one who has picked up a deck of cards in the past and felt that they did not gel, or that they were unable to answer more than just one type of question. Before you draw a single line or start to experiment in Photoshop, it is often useful to create a dummy deck. Whether you write the titles on playing cards or small pieces of paper does not matter. What is important is that you ask questions of your oracle and see how the cards combine and respond. This is a vital stage because it is at this point that titles can be modified or eliminated. If a card does not feel right or appears too vague, you might want to rethink or discard it.

As I have illustrated in some of my examples, cards can be read in combination and this can really ignite the intuition and get ideas and visions forming in your mind. For instance, *Tree* might speak of the importance of family in a one-card-draw but when joined with something else, such as *Snake*, it might point to an untrustworthy family member. It is only when we play about with the cards (or, in this case, our dummy deck) that we can see just how useful it is going to be. Of course, it is possible to take a series of pictures and just add titles without any prior consideration — this has been known to work — but a really well-thought-out deck will most likely have greater value and uses to the user.

You may wonder why I have dedicated so much space to the planning of an oracle. This is a part of the creation process that can often be lacking or neglected entirely. If we return to the idea of the oracle as being like a book, or even a film, the better of these are the ones that have really been considered, with a sturdy narrative and all the characters fleshed out.

DESIGNING YOUR ORACLE

Contents

For most of us, the designing of an oracle is the fun part of the process. It is, after all, the images that many readers connect with, though I believe the titles to be as important for the usability of a deck. In this chapter, we will look at some of the ways in which an oracle deck can be visually designed. This will include how the cards might manifest as a physical tool and, eventually, ways in which they can be printed.

One of the reasons why I wanted to write this book was to dispel the myth that only certain kinds of people (namely those with traditional artistic ability) can create an oracle or tarot deck. Over the years that I have been involved with card reading and creation, it's this perception of what artistic ability is that has continued to put people off. I could not tell you how many times I have heard someone say: "I'd love to create a deck, but I cannot draw."

In my own experience as a designer, I spent a number of years as an art practitioner. Helping many students, from very young children to those in higher and further education, I would visit different schools and deliver workshops relating to design. I have guided students in the creation of their own t-shirt prints, planning murals and have helped them put together group art installations within public spaces. One of the workshops I most enjoyed providing over the years was based around the identity of the students themselves, encouraging them to create a variety of art cards inspired by their personalities and experiences. These would include things they were excited to speak about but also those parts of themselves they might find easier to express through image and without words. Of course, the 'I can't draw' scenario arose on many occasions, so different methods of creation were found. Some of these will be explored in this chapter.

The point being: there are many ways to create a deck without having to put pen, or paintbrush, to paper.

CONVEYING MEANING

One of the most important facets of an oracle deck is being able to convey mood through an image. A little time spent considering how it can be done will benefit both the designer and the user. And it's not nearly as difficult as it might seem.

Think for a minute or two about how you might convey peace or calm within a card. You might want to include a body of water. Might the water then be more suggestive of calm if it is still and lightly touched by the sun than if it is choppy beneath a cloudy sky? Cards which act as a warning may be created in darker tones, with pointed or spiky shapes rather than curves in their construction.

FOR EXAMPLE, CALM...

Style can also convey mood. Modern, brash, or simplistic design will read differently to mystical or antique styles of art — and will also appeal to different kinds of people. There are many decks on the market built around the Fae and fairies, but their styles divide them. Whereas some are light and hopeful, others play on the mischievous tales of the faerie realm. While both dealing with essentially the same topic, the way in which the artist has developed the mood makes them quite different reading experiences. When you're developing a style for your deck, therefore, you can look to your theme for inspiration, meaning you can tailor the visual language to the narrative you want to convey.

Below:
The New Chapter Tarot, Briggs, K.
Mystical Medleys: A Vintage Cartoon Tarot, Hall, G.

COLOR MEANINGS

Color is an extremely important aspect of an oracle deck. Color palettes communicate mood and theme while also tying the cards together. It is not only the original artist who will need to think before choosing their palette: the creator who uses pre-existing art will have the same decisions to make.

People react to color in different ways: your chosen palette can soothe one viewer while invoking a passionate response in others. How color is used in our everyday surroundings will add to the associations with that color in the reader's mind. Because of their use in road signs, red will make us stop while green allows us to go. Think of the taps on your bath: in this case, red tells us that the water will be hot, and blue suggests it is cold. In the natural world, color can act as a warning to deter predators, highlighting food we shouldn't eat or animals that must not be approached. Yellow, in the natural world, is a warning of danger — but it's also the color of the sun and is associated with warmth and even invitation. And of course, people originating from different cultures will also view color in different ways.

Regardless of these different connotations, what follows is a brief look at color and its traditional, spiritual symbolism.

Page Left: *The Cosmic Slumber Tarot,* Walden, T.

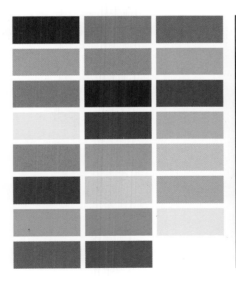

Red has high visibility, which is why it is used for warning signs and as a deterrent. It can raise the blood pressure, and suggests anger and battles in some decks, connecting the color to fire and blood. In some cards, it might be used for red-hot passion, linking the color to intensity and excitement. The symbol for a heart is often red, as is a rose, igniting love and true feeling in the viewer.

KEYWORDS: rage, intensity, passion, lust, strength, anger, battle, danger, love

Green is often predominant in card decks associated with nature (thanks to its abundance in plant life and the natural landscape) and is, therefore, a soothing color to the eye. This is why it is often used for pharmaceuticals and medical packaging. The color is related to healing, and those decks built around angels will often use it in connection with Archangel Raphael, a figure associated with healthcare. The snake — a symbol of Asclepius, Greek god of medicine — is also usually green in oracle decks, to evoke this specific meaning. Green can be suggestive of growth and peace. And yet, green is also the color of envy. The shade of green you use can help you pinpoint which meaning you want to communicate.

KEYWORDS: healing, refreshment, luck, growth, jealousy, nature

Within some card decks, yellow is associated with mental activity and the element of air. It can be representative of clarity and clear thought. When used with consideration in an oracle deck, it can promote warmth and vitality. *The Sun* card from the tarot will oftentimes be saturated in yellow hues, suggesting cheerfulness and energy. Flashes of lightning in the tarot are also colored yellow, making it the color of emergency and change — but also of radiance and divine inspiration.

KEYWORDS: warmth, good health, change, inspiration, radiance, mental activity

Blue can be a cooling color and, within the natural landscape, can be seen in the sky, the ocean and even glimpsed in ice. In advertising, it is used to depict cleanliness and purity. It can also be used as an appetite suppressant and is not usually associated with food design. Blue can be representative of wisdom and knowledge, and is linked to the masculine.

KEYWORDS: coolness, cleanliness, contemplation, sincerity, patience, understanding

Orange is not unlike yellow and some of the meanings — such as cheerfulness and vitality — will apply to both. Health is often associated with the color, as are vitamins, and it can stimulate the appetite for this reason. The season of autumn is also relevant, making this a color of harvest and abundance.

KEYWORDS: plenty, warmth, health, good mood, exuberance

Within card decks, purple is often aligned with royalty, whether this pertains to the color of clothing that is worn or even the borders surrounding specific cards. It often has a mystical feel to it and can be connected to ethereal wisdom or experience. There is an air of superiority and luxury to the color purple, and hints of such might become part of the more magical or otherworldly aspects of your deck. In some cases, the color might denote depression or loneliness.

KEYWORDS: nobility, royalty, the mystical, mystique, wisdom, loneliness

Pink, not unlike red, can be associated with love, though its softness lends itself more to romance than passion. With its gentle hues, it is approachable and harmonious, hinting at affection. Notably, it is a color associated with young girls and is therefore connected to femininity. It is often used to communicate playfulness and youth.

Specific shades of pink are often in vogue — dusty pinks and rose gold, for instance, have been notably on trend for the past few years. Other pinks, like salmon, have become increasingly prevalent in masculine clothing despite the color's feminine associations. Color, after all, is not gender. You can use color to align with social ideas, or to subvert them!

KEYWORDS: playfulness, romance, sweetness, femininity, friendship, affection, fashion, social norms

As an absence of light, the color black is often used in card decks to symbolize the more shadowy aspects of life and, naturally, death. It is associated with the unknown and is, quite obviously, a reflection of inner fear, gloom and anxiety. Therefore, the color can be used in cards relating to grief and mourning. In a deck of cards, black can be used to great effect, since it is also stylish and elegant when mixed with other colors, such as red or yellow.

KEYWORDS: death, fear, depth, gloom, feeling blocked, negativity, elegance, style

White is symbolic of purity and innocence — think 'pure as driven snow'. Symbolically linked with the dove, it communicates peace and tranquility. Many deck creators will use this color to invoke the idea of new beginnings, spiritual connection, and angels. Used within the medical world, white conveys feelings of cleanliness and sterility.

KEYWORDS: purity, innocence, peace, cleanliness, spirit, youth

The color of earth, chocolate, and wood, brown is connected to nature, warmth, comfort, and groundedness. You could use it to denote dirt, or to create an inviting, homely image. It combines well with other warm colors like reds, yellows, and oranges, but also makes blue more vibrant.

KEYWORDS: warmth, earth, dirt, nature, comfort, groundedness

Color combinations can be useful too, and this is something to consider. We have already seen the opposing significance of red and green in a road sign when viewed from a vehicle, but using the colors together can also be suggestive of Christmas and winter (holly berries and pine, for instance). If red accompanies black, it can symbolize 'the enemy', a startling color combination that dominates the posters of many horror or suspense films.

For tarot decks, many artists and publishers choose to color-code the suits. In my own deck, *Spirit Within Tarot*, I chose to color each suit in shades of the same hue, in line with my understanding of the elements — the Cups (water) were painted in variations of blue, the Wands (fire) are in a burnt orange, the Swords (air) are in yellows and the Pentacles (earth) are grounded in natural greens. Within a large reading, this kind of color-coding or palette design can help a reader to immediately recognize which suit (or element) dominates or is missing. This method is employed by many creators, helping define which cards are deemed positive or negative.

Wands

Cups

Swords

Pentacles

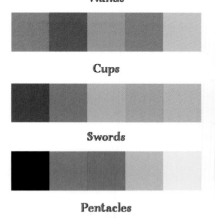

KNIGHT *of* WANDS — KNIGHT *of* CUPS — KNIGHT *of* SWORDS — KNIGHT *of* PENTACLES

Above: *Modern Witch Tarot,* Sterle, L.

96

THE SYMBOLIC APPROACH

Not all creators approach the design of an oracle deck in the literal way shown in previous examples: some choose to use symbols as a way of delivering their messages. For example, to visually evoke the meaning of the title of *Solution*, they might wish to include a key on the card. Symbols are an easy means of tapping into the unconscious mind. The idea of a key, whether written as a word or depicted as an image, is relatable to most people and will effortlessly conjure up the idea of unlocking boxes or opening secret rooms. Similarly, most people will see a fox as being cunning and therefore indicating craftiness.

Creating an oracle with symbols is a popular approach and can add an air of mystery to the deck, giving it a language all its own. You can combine symbols within one card to encode it with meaning. This will help the reader immediately understand what it means, and intuitively interpret how it applies to the question they've asked without having to look in a booklet. Conversely, you can also create a deck (like the Lenormand) constructed of cards with only one symbol. This can make for flexible yet pragmatic readings, as symbol cards drawn together start to tell a story through their combined meanings.

What follows is a short directory of 37 symbols to give you an idea of how a symbolic oracle might be crafted. You can be as creative as you like with your choice of references, but the following suggest some of the more popular ones.

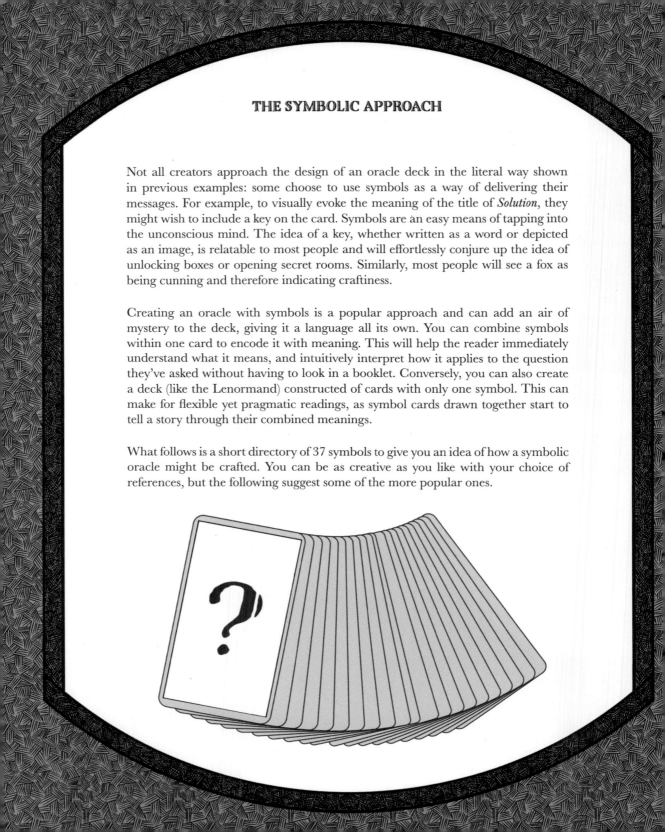

ANCHOR:

The anchor has been used many times throughout history as a symbol. It's sometimes referred to as a token of hope in Christianity and, more obviously, in association with the sailor. Due to its purpose — a weight used to slow or 'anchor' a boat — it often symbolizes stability. Within the Lenormand, this is much the case, and is suggestive of resilience and the laying of foundations. When it appears in a reading, the Lenormand *Anchor* card can speak of durability and strength, much like the origin of the symbol in tattoo art.

In general oracles, the anchor symbol is perceived in much the same way as in the Lenormand cards. However, at times, its shadow interpretations can suggest being stuck, or a person being stubborn. As a card of movement, it is going nowhere fast. As with all cards, it takes combinations to shed light on the true meaning. When combined with *Dog*, it suggests someone who will stick with you through both the good and bad times — a lifelong friend, perhaps. With *Heart*, we find someone who is romantically faithful, loyal or even, sometimes, someone who feels trapped in a relationship that is going nowhere.

BED:

A bed can suggest different things to different people. For some, it will be symbolic of rest, showing up to encourage a good night's sleep, or to warn them that they are overdoing things. In readings where someone is experiencing health difficulties, it might highlight anything from being pulled out of action by the common cold to convalescing in hospital.

The bed can be a tricky symbol because of the many different meanings attributed to it. For some it will represent sex but there will also be others who will be put in mind of the old adage 'you made your bed and now you must lie in it', suggesting karma and consequence. It is important to set your parameters around the card: the design of this image will become a large part of how it is interpreted, should you decide to use the symbol. A bed for sleep and a bed for lovemaking may look quite different through the lens of an oracle.

ANT:

An ant is often considered to be a worker. Carrying more than its own body weight, it might represent strength and dedication — but the enthusiasm that the insect puts into combining its energy with that of others means that it can be connected to teamwork in an oracle, too. In a tarot deck, the ant might be used to describe the *Three of Pentacles*, a card sometimes considered to mean 'joint effort' in the *Rider-Waite-Smith* system.

BLACK CAT:

While black cats are often regarded as a trusty familiar of the witch, much of Europe has learned to view the animal as a negative omen. We are told that should a black cat cross our path bad luck will befall us. How you choose to use this symbol is very much up to your own set of beliefs and the way in which you view the animal. Many see the cat as a symbol of magic and power. In Scotland and Ireland, the arrival of a black cat at your home can suggest prosperity, luck, and wishes coming true. However, if the superstition of misfortune and mystery is ingrained within your understanding of this symbol, it could act as a warning for a spell of bad luck being just around the corner.

BOOT:

The boot, within my own experience as a reader, is a symbol of authority, command and, sometimes, domination. Within the tarot deck, these attributes fall at the feet of *The Emperor*; some depictions of the archetype, such as that of the *Tarot Nova*, are shown as a boot. As an example, you might think of the tarot Emperor as stamping his foot in order to get what he wants.

This connection to dominance is not an entirely new way of looking at the symbol. Since WWI, the boot has repeatedly been used to suggest military aggression and oppression, which is reflected in our terminology — think of someone being 'under the heel'. But the image can also cause us to think of those things we might wish to crush under the sole of our shoe. More recently, the boot of the dominatrix comes to mind: an expression of desirable superiority and consensual control. The distinction between these meanings can be denoted visually by the type of boot you use: a combat boot would relate to authority and the military; a steel-capped boot could mean oppression, or could be seen as an inoffensive work boot; a stiletto-heeled boot would evoke the dominatrix interpretation.

BOOK:

A book can be symbolic of knowledge. Within its pages, it holds information and can therefore refer to learning and education. Within the Lenormand system, the book is representative of secrets and, when closed, can speak of material that may be relevant but is presently unknown. Alternatively, if the book is open, then its contents are available for use. If you use this symbol, consider how you would like it to work in your readings. Does it offer information that will be beneficial and that is accessible to the reader? Or is it descriptive of withheld information which could change a situation once it is unveiled?

BOX:

A box can come in many shapes and sizes. For some, it will be the symbol of a gift, wrapped in attractive paper and finished with a bow. For others, it is suggestive of those things that are hidden. In dream symbolism, the box is considered to contain secrets that the dreamer is holding back from those around them. From childhood stories, we can all remember the enticingly dusty old boxes hidden away in attics, filled with magical or illuminating objects. More often than not, they have great significance to the plot once discovered. If we think of Pandora in Greek mythology, however, the opening of that box could prove to have dire consequences.

In a reading, a box could represent all of the aforementioned, but it might be just as insightful to hand the card to the reader and ask them what they think is concealed inside. Their response could be extremely interesting within the scope of the reading and might even be the key to helping them to move forward. Because of symbols' psychological associations, this is how oracle decks can help readers unlock answers within themselves: what they see within a symbol informs their interpretation of the card.

BROKEN VASE:

A vase might symbolize something ornate or grand that is held in high regard, but when it has been broken it can suggest loss. While smashed pottery can be glued back together, it rarely looks the same as it did originally; within your oracle, a broken vase is reminiscent of those experiences or losses that cannot be easily repaired — if at all. Relationships may have fallen apart, or trust has been irrevocably destroyed.

CAGE:

The symbol of the cage is quite obvious in its meaning. Cages are used to restrict and confine. While the idea of physically caging an animal or person might seem cruel and abusive, when used in a deck of cards, the cage more likely represents mental limitation or low confidence. This might concern a lack of imagination in more creative readings, but could also, within the context of unbalanced relationships, reflect feelings of powerlessness. It is not unusual for people to stay in bad relationships because their partner has led them to believe that they'll never find anyone else.

When self-confidence is low, it makes breaking out of a mental prison such as this much harder.

On a mundane level, the cage can represent delays or anything that restricts a person's freedom. As an example, a lack of relevant qualifications will restrict someone from a career that requires specific certification.

101

CLOVER:

In the Lenormand system, *Clover* is a token of luck; in fact, because of its size, the Lenormand *Clover* grants 'small luck' rather than grand fortune. Like many, you may have searched for the infamous four-leaf clover in the hope of your wishes being granted, but Irish tradition actually states that should you find a five-leaf clover, even greater success and financial luck will be yours.

When the clover, be it four or five-leafed, enters a reading, it offers prosperity. This could be suggestive of a stroke of good luck or an opportunity.

COIN:

A coin is representative of money and, therefore, will signify finances within a reading. When alone, it can suggest the receiving of some amount of money, but the card will likely make more sense in combination with others. If it appears in combination with crossroads imagery, the choice of two different investments might be relevant. When accompanied by a letter, a cheque is forthcoming. The Lenormand and Kipper decks root these symbols to individual cards, while the tarot combines many symbols in one card to give a nuanced meaning. If you wanted a card to mean *Financial Stability,* you could use coins along with the anchor symbol.

COFFIN:

Not unlike the *Death* card in tarot, the symbol of the coffin is often feared. But like the thirteenth trump of the tarot deck, it rarely depicts death proper; instead, it is a harbinger of endings.

The coffin appears in both the Lenormand and Kipper systems but is only titled as such in the former. In the latter it is named *Fatality*. Most likely, the card will bring about something irrevocable like retirement or redundancy, the end of a relationship, or being stripped of a title or position. This is not, of course, meant to sugar-coat the symbol. The coffin can, in extreme situations, foretell the passing of a loved one, but these predictions might not be as unexpected as you imagine. It is important to remember that when the cards foretell a death — one which you may *not* have seen coming — the coffin is unlikely to turn up on its own. More often, the turning of a card that features the coffin symbol will be less significant than you fear.

CORNUCOPIA:

The cornucopia is the classic horn of plenty, symbolic of nourishment. Originally regarded as the horn of the goat broken off by Heracles during battle, the cornucopia is associated with both the goddess Fortuna and the concept of fortune. It is often shown as a horn-shaped receptacle filled with fruits, vegetables and flowers, heralding great abundance for the seeker in an oracle reading.

It might be natural to see this simply as a card of financial gain. Rather, the cornucopia is a symbol of good health, vitality, and joy. Associated with the season of autumn, it is also connected to a productive harvest. In short, the symbol is representative of fulfillment — be that romantic, spiritual, or that of upcoming financial security.

DOG:

Within the Lenormand tradition, the *Dog* card is a symbol of friendship and faithfulness — something which carries over in a general oracle deck. When close to a character card, it will help you to see who can be trusted and will have your back. The dog is regarded as 'man's best friend' and, within your oracle, could refer to someone who is loyal. Only when partnered with a card such as the *Fox* (which is linked to deviousness and cunning) will the *Dog* be less devoted and steadfast. A false friend could be hinted at when this duo turns up in a reading. In the tarot, the dog also relates to domesticity. The *Moon* card depicts a dog and wolf in a wild landscape, contrasting the controlled, domestic world (referred to by the dog) with an untamed, natural state of being (evoked by the wolf). Again, this is how you can combine symbols within one card to provide a detailed meaning.

CROSSROADS:

Crossroads are commonly thought to depict a time of decision-making. With two paths to choose from, the crossroads ask that the seeker make a choice between them. In many cultures, the crossroads are considered to be a doorway, offering transition to another phase or stage of life. This would make sense should you consider the fact that each decision we make comes with its own consequences. When you choose a path at the crossroads, you must accept what you find along that road.

Within the oracle deck, the forked road suggests two different opportunities. While these might be lifechanging, we encounter decisions every day, whether that's which route we take on our way to work or how we choose to react to a problem or situation. The *Crossroads* prompts us to examine these choices and consider which would be the most beneficial. In a reading, it might alert you to more options than you initially thought you had.

DOVE:

The dove has distinctly contrasting meanings in different cultures and parts of the world. In ancient Germany, the bird was regarded as a symbol of spirit but also of death. However, the dove is most often assumed to represent peace, most likely due to the three birds let out by Noah after the great flood in the Bible. Returning with an olive branch in its beak, the dove symbolized a reconciliation with God and, therefore, has since become a token of truce.

Within the structure of the oracle, peace is a welcome sign, especially for anyone who feels as though they have been through an ordeal. Like the dove of Christianity, a card like this can bring much comfort during or just after a stormy period.

EGG:

The egg is symbolic of new beginnings. If we think about the eggs gifted at Easter, we understand that they are symbols of resurrection, but prior to the Christian holiday, the egg is also thought to have been a symbol of new life and of spring, linked to the Germanic goddess Eostre who is connected to fertility.

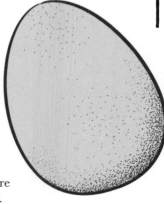

The egg, as symbol in an oracle, is all about potential. It is equivalent to the seed or sapling pushing its way up through the earth and starting anew. Within the egg is the potential of life and all of its possibilities. When it is turned in a reading, the egg suggests a new start and — if the right cards are present — news of a birth. Only when accompanied by symbols such as the coffin will it have negative connotations of something ending before it has begun — or it might give the hopeful meaning of an ending leading to a new start.

EAR:

The ear symbolizes one of our five senses: the ability to hear. In an oracle, it asks us to listen and recommends that we pay attention. Is there something of importance that we might have missed? Are we likely to lose out on a prime opportunity because we have become distracted and unfocused? In a sense, the ear is an alarm call. Sometimes, we only hear what we want to, and this symbol could ask that we broaden our attention. Combined with symbolism like the book, a card could utilize the ear symbol to encourage the reader to listen, as important information is there for the taking.

FOX:

The *Fox* is understood within some schools of Lenormand readers to be sneaky and untrustworthy. The idea of a 'fox in the henhouse' has meant that people see the animal as devious and only out for himself. Japanese folklore considers the fox, or kitsune, to be a trickster spirit who will mislead you — many Native American folk tales also characterize the fox in this way.

These cultural associations have led to the fox being used within some of the more dubious cards within the tarot. You will sometimes see him in the *Seven of Swords* (a card of deceit) or symbolizing the *Page of Swords* (sometimes thought of as a spy). However, not everyone likes the negative interpretations attributed to the fox and some see the animal as merely astute when it comes to looking out for himself and his family. After all, the fox is also thought of as being cunning.

However you view the animal, the symbol of the fox is one to watch out for in your oracle: he will always inform readings, especially in relation to the other cards that are drawn alongside one that includes him. It could mean that someone around you can't be trusted, or that maybe it's time to think of 'number one' and look out for your own interests.

GRAMOPHONE:

In my own oracles — those that I have made just for myself — the gramophone is my card of fun and getting together with others. In some oracle decks, such a card might be entitled Music, but the essence is much the same: a time to get together with friends and enjoy yourself.

In a predictive sense, the symbol of a gramophone could suggest that a party or social occasion is on the cards. This would likely be something informal, such as a night out or a spontaneous get-together. As an answer to a question about what you could do in the present, it may be suggesting that you let your hair down and have a good time. For those seeking love, the symbol might suggest that their perfect partner can be found through friends or met at a social event of some kind.

GLOBE:

The most obvious interpretation of the globe is travel. Many designers use the symbol, quite understandably, in *The World* card of the tarot, suggesting the end of a cycle or the concept of completion. The globe also makes an appearance in the *Two of Wands*, symbolizing planning and forward thinking. For many, both of these cards hint at overseas travel and vacations.

On a deeper level, the globe could be asking the reader to consider the bigger picture. Sometimes, we can become so wrapped up in the finer details of our lives that we miss the greater plan. This symbol might ask for you to think ahead or think bigger than you currently are. The globe is the symbol of visionaries rather than those who are fearful of expanding their perspective and upping their game.

HEART:

The heart has had an association with both love and emotions for a long time. Most often seen on Valentine's Day cards and, more recently, as an emoji or symbol of 'liking' something on social media platforms, it is generally regarded as a positive image. In fact, most people enjoy seeing a card relating to love turn up in a reading since it suggests new romance, an admirer, or the stabilization of a current relationship. The heart is used in the Lenormand as a sign of romantic intention. However, away from cards of positive unions, the symbol has been adopted to depict betrayal and heartache in the tarot deck — the *Three of Swords* shows it pierced by three blades, bleeding beneath a stormy sky.

Most renderings of the heart are uplifting in nature, however within an oracle its presence brings thoughts of deep bonds and emotional fulfillment to mind. When mixed with other symbols, you can lock the heart down to a chosen meaning. By combining the heart symbol with a globe, a long-distance affair is implied, or it may indicate that someone might be admiring you from afar. Combined with a fox, a lover might be unfaithful or insincere; with a ring, a proposal of marriage or greater commitment may be upon you. You can also separate these symbols out into separate cards to allow for flexibility in a reading, rather than prescribing exactly which connotation of the heart symbol you mean.

HOUSE:

The *House* can describe someone's security, as much as the place in which they live. Because the symbolic title omits the warmth of it being a home, this card could be more about the physical

structure of a building. With money symbology, it could propose structural repairs or refurbishment; when paired with a dove, possibly retreat.

It is more likely to focus on the actual home when partnered with a symbol like the heart ('home is where the heart is', or the idea of a love-nest) or a tree (somewhere that protects the family).

HOURGLASS:

The importance of time in the oracle has already been mentioned and the hourglass can act as a symbol of such. Whereas some cards will advise that things will take longer than expected or that we must learn the lesson of tolerance, the hourglass is a sure sign that time is always passing and might even be running out. Whether this symbol highlights a deadline that is getting nearer, or the fears a seeker might have about starting a family later in life, the context of the question will play a big part in how time has a bearing on the issue.

KEY:

A key is a symbol of power, for it allows the owner to unlock something. Mystery and confusion can be dispelled when the key is on a card, because it allows what is unknown to become known — it is the keys on the tarot's *Hierophant* card that specifically suggest that the reader can access the hierarchy of knowledge that is packed into the card's other symbolic imagery.

Keys are more often used to describe the opening or unlocking of something, rather than the locking or shutting out of something — but how you place this symbol on your card can dictate which of these connotations is intended. Even direction can make a difference: a key facing towards the reader might hint at them unlocking something within, while a key facing away from the reader would be inviting them to unlock something outside themselves.

LETTER:

The *Letter* concerns mail. In this day and age, this includes more than the physical mail that comes through the letterbox. It also includes email. This symbol could broadly denote communication, but more specifically you can use it to imply written communication or a message from one person to another. And again, you can combine symbols to tailor a card's meaning. With coins, financial papers will be relevant; with a gramophone, the letter could be a social invitation; with a heart, a love letter or Valentine's Day card might be on the way.

LIGHT BULB:

A light bulb is often associated with bright ideas. In modern culture, it is sometimes shown hovering above someone's head when they've had an epiphany. In an oracle deck, the emergence of the light bulb might suggest clarity or some kind of realization, leading the reader to believe that something will soon become clear or that a new thought process or idea has potential.

LOCKET:

Lockets are usually placed on a chain and kept close to the heart. Within them, one usually keeps photos of loved ones or even a lock of hair. The locket, in the oracle, is centered on memories and nostalgia.

Due to our understanding of memories, if you use this symbol within your oracle it is likely to represent a distant remembering, rather than the remembrance of things that have happened recently, though this is dependent on the subject and timeframe of the reading. When partnered with a symbol like the key, it would suggest that the answer to a problem can be found in a person or situation from the past. With the heart, an ex-lover may return, or you might be finding it hard to move on from a previous relationship.

MASK:

The mask conceals. On a general level, it suggests that something may not be as it seems. The essence of this symbol is similar to how we think of the light of the moon: it highlights some of what is there but, in doing so, plunges everything else into the shadows. In this sense, it makes us aware of those things that cannot be seen and asks that we consider the possibility that the whole truth of a situation is not immediately apparent.

This is a useful symbol because it can, at times, confirm a seeker's fears. As a direct response to the question 'what do I need to know?' the mask suggests that something is being covered up, or that someone is purposely holding back information. If used on a character card, a masked person would imply that they have a different intention to that which they present. Or perhaps they're just putting on an act, while their true self lies beneath the mask?

MAGNIFYING GLASS:

We have already seen that the globe symbol offers a bigger-picture mindset — 'don't sweat the small stuff' but think from a broader perspective. However, there will be times when the opposite is true: focusing in on the details might be just as important within a host of different scenarios.

The magnifying glass can remind us to focus in on the particulars. If this symbol is combined with that of the letter, then the card is recommending that we examine the small print of a contract. With a ring, we are being asked to look at the everyday things that a partner does for us rather than the grand gestures.

RING:

The ring is a symbol of partnership, though not necessarily an unwavering commitment unless joined with a symbol such as the anchor, indicating a steadfast support and a watertight bond. As an oracle card, the ring suggests the coming-together of two people or things, though this need not always be a romantic connection. Rings can highlight all kinds of bonds, from business partnerships to legal contracts. Other symbols will always provide extra information and must not be ignored: when appearing with a coffin, a union is ending; with a letter, some kind of proposal or agreement is indicated.

SNAKE:

The snake is one of the oldest and most widespread symbols in mythology. Whether it is known as magical or malevolent very much depends on where you come from.

The snake is well known as a symbol of transformation due to the shedding of its skin, but in some schools of Lenormand thought, it is the snake's bite that has given it a personality within the cards. Because of the playing card association (*Queen of Clubs*), the Lenormand *Snake* can sometimes refer to a woman we must be cautious and wary of. This interpretation — of someone appearing slippery or unpredictable — has followed through into some oracle decks,

though there are others that concentrate on the idea of renewal and self-care. As we've seen before, the Greeks associated the snake with medicine, while in Christian theology it is associated with rebellion from the divine.

SCISSORS:

As opposed to the joining of two things, the symbol of the scissors represents separation. It cuts us off from something, sometimes relieving us of pain and providing freedom. As an oracle card, the Scissors is a much-needed player. It can warn us of those things that are soon to be dissolved; it can also suggest relationships or interactions that no longer serve a purpose or could be affecting our wellbeing. It would be easy to think of this as being only connected to toxic or unworthy partners, but the card might also hint at personal habits that need to be culled or a lifestyle we've outgrown.

SPIDER:

The spider might strike fear into the hearts of some, but her meaning within the oracle has little to do with arachnophobia. Rather, it is the web that helps most to divine meaning from the creature. Due to the spider's resourcefulness, most of us are in awe of its creativity, precision and determination.

Regardless of weather conditions, we watch the spider build and continually attend to its web, showing perseverance and commitment. This has led to it symbolizing effort and a strong work ethic. With a symbol such as the ring beside it, you might witness someone who takes a partnership seriously and is prepared to work at making things right. When in combination with a key, the solution to a problem would likely involve rolling up your sleeves and getting on with the task at hand. Symbolically, the spider's web can be seen as a token of connections with others — maybe even via the internet or the 'world-wide web'.

TELEPHONE:

The telephone is a means of communication. Unlike the letter, which we have already encountered, this most likely refers to aural communication. Speaking over the telephone is the most obvious example, due to the symbolism used, but any kind of spoken dialogue is noted when this card arrives in a reading.

The letter symbol might be viewed as a more formal means of connection, meaning that the telephone can refer, at times, to everyday conversation. This would mean, in some circumstances, that not everything passed on is correct. Tittle-tattle, scandal, gossip and lies could be foretold, should a snake or fox be close by.

STAR:

The image of the star, or stars, exists within both the tarot and Lenormand decks. Not surprisingly, the tarot version is connected to hope and guidance. Due to the ordering of tarot's Major Arcana, *The Star* is often related to optimism after difficult times. Within many oracles, the tarot meaning has filtered through, highlighting the star as a token of inspiration and hopefulness for the future. If you think of the night sky as a metaphor, it can sometimes take the darkness of night (and, indeed, human experience) to help us see what is truly important, and the twinkling stars are emblems of this.

TREE:

The tree is associated with health in the Lenormand deck, but personally, I prefer to link it to the Family in an oracle. This might bring the idea of the family tree to mind, each with its own branches. Families often stretch out far and wide, geographically as well as emotionally. Despite our possible differences with blood-ties, the roots pull us all together, even if only on paper.

Within an oracle, Tree would suggest that family is relevant, if not important. When connected to a 'person card', it would highlight ties through blood or marriage. With *Money*, an inheritance might perhaps be indicated. The tree is often associated with great strength and might inspire you to think about stability within your family, both near and far.

WHAT DO THE CARDS MEAN TO YOU?

Pick a meaning for your card and use this space to construct a mind map around it. Think about what you associate with this meaning. It may help to group your mind map into these aspects: symbols, imagery, title, keywords, number, color, emotions.

I created this mind map when I was brainstorming my version of The Hermit:

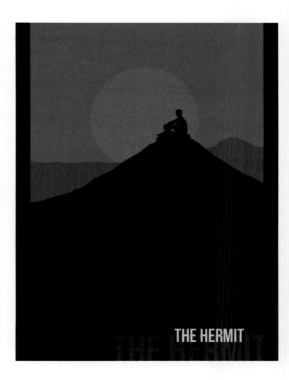

Above: *The Spirit Within Tarot.* Bright, S.

Try it here :

METHODS OF ORACLE CREATION

The methods of oracle creation are vast in range, regardless of any artistic limitations you may feel that you have. Some creators will naturally know where their strengths lie and will gravitate towards a specific area of expertise. For others, it might take longer to find the right fit. It is perfectly normal for a creator to try more than one option during the experimental phase, trying out different styles and methods so that they can ascertain which is the most successful. A specific subject or theme may, perhaps, suit photography even if you are a keen and experienced painter.

The following examples are methods which have been tried and tested by creators who have already walked this path. Through their experience and wisdom, I hope you'll find an approach that will suit your own creative needs.

Below: Photography by Loveday, M.
Page Right Stamps: *The New Chapter Tarot*
Special Limited Edition, Briggs, K.

USING PRE-EXISTING ARTWORK

Creators and publishers will, on occasion, use a portfolio of existing work and tie the right images to the right cards. You can pull from your own work or use that of another artist. Pictures will tell their own stories, which allows the oracle creator to swiftly build up a deck based on whatever meanings they can find in the pre-existing artwork. Providing that the portfolio of images is diverse, you should be able to put together a broad and usable deck. The artworks of Arthur Rackham, Nicoletta Ceccoli and Victoria Frances have all provided a basis for oracles, with the supporting text and structure fitting around the images rather than the reverse.

This is, as you might guess, easier with an oracle deck than a tarot, since the images used will often dictate the structure of the deck rather than the other way around. For this reason, creating a tarot in this fashion can be a lot harder: finding 78 images within an existing body of work that all successfully relate to the traditional card archetypes can be an ordeal. In some decks, this has led to tenuous connections between image and intended meaning, resulting in cards appearing forced and, therefore, in a weak tarot.

Having said that, there are a few notable exceptions to this rule. *The Da Vinci Enigma Tarot* by Caitlin Matthews is a good example of an instance in which the artwork (from Leonardo da Vinci's sketchbooks) enhances the tarot cards, rather than twisting them away from their traditional meanings. This tarot is not just a catalogue of pretty images: these pieces, meticulously chosen, are a link to the mind and inspirations of Leonardo, but also act as a window into the psyche of the reader or seeker, too.

Author of over 70 books and a selection of tarot and oracle decks, including *The Arthurian Tarot* (with husband and fellow author John Matthews) and *The Ancestral Oracle of the Celts*, Caitlin Matthews is one of the leading authorities on Celtic wisdom and Western mystery traditions. When designing the majority of her decks, Caitlin works with an artist, sometimes drawing out her ideas first and then passing them on to be redrawn or painted by a professional.

Page Left: Photography by Bright, S. Cards from *The New Chapter Tarot*. Briggs, K.

CAITLIN MATTHEWS
Creator of *The Da Vinci Enigma Tarot*

What was the original inspiration behind The Da Vinci Enigma Tarot?

The deck was inspired by an exhibition of Leonardo's machines in an old, disused church in Venice. They were hanging from the ceiling and John and I just looked at each other and wondered why nobody had already done a tarot that showcases Leonardo's art.

What creative process did you go through when creating The Da Vinci Enigma Tarot?

I had the Taschen book about da Vinci, which is one of those vast books, the size of a bible. I also had a biography by Charles Nicholl, *The Flights of the Mind*, which had come out just around that time and was right up to date. I began by looking at the pictures, notebooks, and writings of Leonardo. As many know, he made notes in the margins of his notebooks, writing backwards in a kind of mirror-writing: he'd obviously had a sense of his work not being for everybody to see, which makes the notebooks more intimate than his paintings. He drew in them if he was walking down the street, drawing what he saw, and he'd invent things. He might see an old man in the market and think how perfect he'd be for St Peter and so he'd sketch him.

I really immersed myself in all of it, which is what you do with anything you are creating — you swim in the sea of it. You have to really get to know the subject and material well because, as an example, when a specific picture was unavailable to us, I could swim back into that sea and know where to find a picture that would serve the same purpose.

At the beginning, it was a matter of looking at the images and testing them out. I did a lot of photocopying and worked with a dummy deck because that's the only way you learn if things will work together or not. It is within the playing and using of it that you understand what a deck is capable of.

FOUR *of* AIR
REPOSE

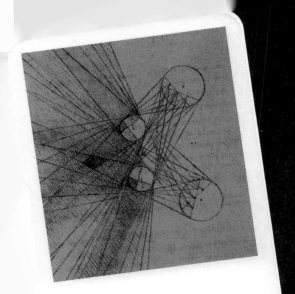

THREE of WATER
CONJUNCTION

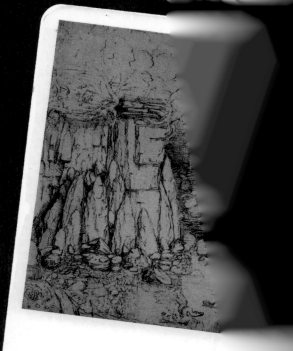

ACE of EARTH
EARTH

DY of AIR

0 FOOL

Did you approach a publisher, or did they contact you?

We always approach publishers. I don't think I have ever done anything where someone said: "Hey, don't you think this would be good for a deck?" We always generate our own ideas, and, in that way, we can keep control over how it works out. Around the time that we had the idea for *The Da Vinci Enigma Tarot*, we would often go for dinner with our publishers; however, we would wait until dessert before laying a new idea on them. Our publisher at the time had very bushy eyebrows and they would rise if an idea was a good one. They disappeared into his hair when we mentioned *The Da Vinci Enigma Tarot* so we knew we were onto something! We were assigned a picture researcher immediately.

What was the publishing process like?

Once the proposal had been sent to a publisher, it was looked at by their board. Depending on the size of the publishing house, there is often only a short amount of time to sell them on the pitch, since yours will not be only the idea on the table. This is why a proposal must be concise so that folk know what the project is about. Not every idea will be looked at, so it is vital that you do your research beforehand and send the right kind of proposal to the right kind of publisher. It is a good idea to look in a bookshop and find the kind of material you wish to have published, then find out who is publishing it and how well distributed it is.

How many co-editions a deck will have is decided on in a board meeting, as well as discussing which languages it will be printed in; the more copies printed, the more affordable they become. Once agreed upon, a contract is then raised, which your agent or author's society can go through with you — should you have one — to make sure that it is fair. The contract should outline what they will do and what you will do, including when the deck and associated written material need to be delivered. This is because it will need to be printed and in the warehouse ready for its release date.

In terms of *The Da Vinci Enigma Tarot*, I was assigned a professional picture researcher who dealt with places like Windsor Castle and the museums. The cards were then printed in China, having [been] designed in-house. They then went directly to the companies and [were] sold on the date of publication.

What difficulties did you run into with The Da Vinci Enigma Tarot?

All of the pictures were in private collections, such as the Royal Collection at Windsor. Some people were very good and got back to us immediately, but some museums were just terrible. When people did not get back in time or even didn't respond, it meant that we could not use the requested images. Nobody refused us the permissions but because we were on a production line, with targets to meet and a date for release, some people responded too late. This meant a few images could not be used.

The Da Vinci Enigma is being reprinted again by Red Feather, Schiffer Publishing, in 2020, and one of the considerations was as to whether we could obtain these permissions again — because when you get reproduction rights for a deck, it doesn't stand for all time. If it were just the same edition being reprinted by the same publisher under the same terms, that would be fine, but because it is being reprinted by a new publishing company, they need to start from scratch and that is at a considerable expense. I was lucky that out of the 78 images requested, about 75 or 76 were the ones I wanted for those particular positions.

There are decks out there that have been made using pre-existing art, but without rights to the pictures it is simply theft. Just because imagery is out there, it doesn't mean that anyone can use it.

Did you decide to change the titles in your deck before you sourced the images or did the images dictate the changes?

Some of the cards in the deck stayed the same, such as *The Fool*, which shows a beggar. However, for *Judgment*, we [used the title of] *Renewal*, which is the function of the card, showing a crowned eagle upon the world. This is, of course, a reference to the Biblical quotation "we will rise up on wings of eagles", meaning that we will be renewed. For a card like *The Star*, I used John the Baptist, whom [we retitled] *The Wayshower*. *The Wayshower* [serves] the function of *The Star* (a wayshower being one who embodies the qualities that he or she wishes to absorb and learn), so I was using names that go with the subject of the picture, but which also have something to do with the meaning of the card. For *The Tower*, I named it *Deluge*, after a flood Leonardo had witnessed in northern Italy. In the examples of the Major Arcana, I found the appropriate images first, which then informed the titles.

What rewards, on a personal level, did you experience from working on this project?

I studied this period of art when I was at school and absolutely loved it, so to have congress with Leonardo's mind, if I can put it that way, was such a privilege. He and I were born exactly [500] years apart: he was born in 1452 and I was born in 1952. It was a different world from ours, but his was waking up in a time when people were not just being guided by religion in a blind way. They were looking at older sources of things. Witnessing da Vinci's inventive eye and mind, at a time when he was at the forefront of new and cutting-edge thinking, was just wonderful.

What advice would you give to someone who is considering compiling pre-existing art for an oracle or tarot?

First of all, if the artwork is by a living artist, speak to them and find out if it is something they would like and how they might be involved. With all artists I work with, we go in 50/50. I think we must always be fair to the artist. If the artist is not living, then check how much a reproduction in World Rights is going to be. For example, I used four images of the *Rider-Waite-Smith* for a book, which cost around £50 each. However, the terms stated that they could only be used for a couple of years, so if your work is likely to stay in print for four or five years, they would want some more money. If your product is going to be published [outside] of your country, then you are going to need World Rights. If you only get permissions for it to be printed in the UK, you are therefore unable to use it in a US edition. Not everyone is set up [financially] to do this. There is no way that I could have afforded to do *The Da Vinci Enigma Tarot* myself.

For anyone wanting to create a deck, I would remind them that it is a long job and to do it properly. Immerse yourself in it and make sure that the concept is right. If the concept is good, make sure that all of the cards fit comfortably under that umbrella. Our imagination can be fertile, but some ideas will only be a quick burn. It is these ideas that you have to test because you can't always tell if they have longevity. We must, therefore, test our stamina and the stamina of the idea.

LICENSE-FREE PHOTOGRAPHY

It is highly unlikely that the majority of us will be able to afford the permissions for high-price artwork such as that of Leonardo da Vinci and other artists — but there are other means of obtaining pre-existing artwork and photography. There are a great many online sites that sell stock imagery for commercial use, and these can prove very useful and financially viable places for deck designers. However, as with anything online, the bigger a resource gets, the harder it is to keep checks on everything that is uploaded, so there will always be some sites where not all of their images will fall under the legal restrictions and responsibilities required for publishing. Having said this, there are some websites that have managed to balance the needs of their photographers with those of their userbase.

Founded in 2013, Unsplash is a website known as an industry-leading visual community. The site, which grew from a humble Tumblr blog, offers inspiring images for millions of creators worldwide that are handpicked by their team and are available for use, free of charge, for commercial or noncommercial purposes. The site boasts over one million curated photographs and a community of 157,866 photographers. It does not matter if you use the images as-is or wish to modify them — Unsplash grants users an irrevocable, nonexclusive worldwide copyright license to download, distribute and alter their photographs.

Carolyn Strug is one designer who used Unsplash to create a tarot deck of her own. Feeling that many people showed off decks that were all much the same on their social media accounts, she thought it might be nice to put together a selection of images she'd chosen herself that were unlike anybody else's. One of her reasons for choosing to do so originated from her use of the standard *Tarot de Marseille. The Rider-Waite-Smith* tradition has been brought up to date many, many times but, in terms of social diversity, the *Tarot de Marseille* has not accepted our changing world as readily. There are of course exceptions, but most versions stay close to its original format.

Carolyn decided to investigate the world of stock photography, mostly because it was a sure way to obtain an instant image. "I didn't have to draw or paint something," she says, "and not having to spend a lot of time on that part of the process allowed me to skip forward with regards to the design." At the time of creating her deck, Carolyn also had another reason for immersing herself in the project. "I was looking for some instant gratification. News about [COVID19] had really ratcheted up that week and was becoming scarier. I needed something to occupy my anxious mind; however, starting a deck from scratch, so to speak, seemed insurmountable. Once I started looking at the available photos online, I started to get really excited about how I could pull together other people's images to represent the card meanings and, once I started doing it, I found it to be fast and easy."

In some cases, Carolyn's initial ideas met with success, but not everything was as accessible. "I'd decided on using matches for the element of fire and swords for air, but finding enough to fill the 40 Minor cards was a challenge. I ended up having to rethink this, using flames for fire and knives, which were easier to find, for the element of air. Finding the right amount for each card was also arduous. I could find two knives for the *Two of Knives* but not the right amount for the *Three or Four*. I would need to build the cards up in another way, showing non-specific but bigger quantities than the one that preceded it, or [working] with the mood of the traditional meaning. For example, the *Five of Cups*, a card associated with loss and sadness, shows only one cup but it is smashed."

Four

Five

Hanged

Magician

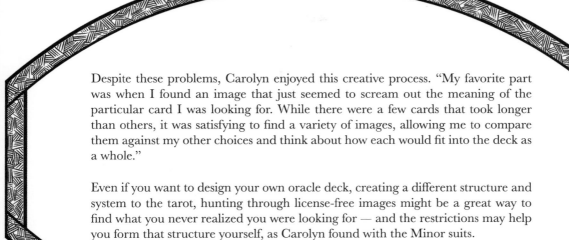

Despite these problems, Carolyn enjoyed this creative process. "My favorite part was when I found an image that just seemed to scream out the meaning of the particular card I was looking for. While there were a few cards that took longer than others, it was satisfying to find a variety of images, allowing me to compare them against my other choices and think about how each would fit into the deck as a whole."

Even if you want to design your own oracle deck, creating a different structure and system to the tarot, hunting through license-free images might be a great way to find what you never realized you were looking for — and the restrictions may help you form that structure yourself, as Carolyn found with the Minor suits.

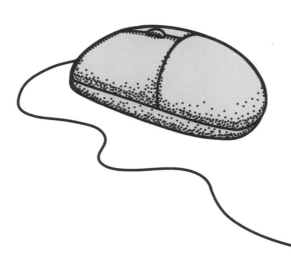

IMAGE HUNT

As a warm-up, why not explore one of these license-free sites? Use keywords associated with your theme to search the site and see what you find. Are any patterns emerging? How do the images relate to each other? Can you weave a story from them?

Using a site with license-free artwork can be a lifeline for those who want to create a deck without designing each card from scratch. It can also allow for the creator to accumulate a vast collection of imagery to pull from. Unless you happen to be well-traveled, you may not have photos in your collection that match the specific scenery you want to portray in your oracle deck. If you want to take your deck out of your everyday surroundings, license-free photography is a great way to integrate scenes from around the world!

As well as free sites like Unsplash, there are also stock library websites where photography can be bought singly or in bundles. DeviantArt is one of the most well-known. Usually, artists who are advertised on the site can be contacted via email; the consumer will explain the details of their project and find out how an image can be purchased. Arrangements will depend on the seller: some will allow their image to be used free of charge, others will want upfront payment. There will be those who are willing to wait until the deck is released and may request a copy. In some cases, trust has been built up between designer and seller, leading to an ongoing trade of images and advertising.

Deposit Photos is a paid site where a subscription can be bought to use photography commercially. While a host of photographs can be found to enhance and construct your images, there are also many figure references online too, showing models in different positions and costumes. These kinds of photosets (which can cover all sorts of different subject matter, from people to animals to weaponry) can be useful if you don't have a great deal of people around you. Some decks can require many different characters and this kind of resource will enable a greater scope for diversity. Similarly, sites for backgrounds are also popular since a desired scene might not be readily obtainable. For the more fantastical and elaborate decks, specific photographic backdrops, which appear to be out of this world, have already been created for the use of designers.

Left: *Modern Witch Tarot Coloring Book*, Sterle, L.
Above: *The Mountain Dream Tarot*, Nettles, B.

THE POSTCARD ORACLE

Page Right Stamps: *The New Chapter Tarot - Special Limited Edition, Briggs, K.*

As long as a creator is not considering reprinting, one way of creating an oracle using pre-existing art is by compiling an oracle of postcards. The postcard oracle consists of assembled pieces, whether purchased individually or as a set.

The standard size for a postcard is 6 x 4 inches (158 x 105mm). While quite large, cards this size will shuffle as comfortably as the larger oracle decks available from mainstream publishers. Most postcards on sale will adhere to these exact dimensions and therefore fit together well in a deck. These days, postcards are often sold in boxes of 100 or less. This makes it easy to base an oracle around a theme since they are usually grouped by subject matter. For example, the Royal Horticultural Society released a deck of 100 botanical images from the RHS Lindley Libraries in 2013, including rare prints and unusual plants from around the world. Flower oracles have grown in popularity thanks to the fact that meanings have been assigned to many species, and researching potential interpretations for different cards can prove to be a rich, rewarding, and educational experience when compiling such a deck.

While the bulk-buy option will appeal to some, there will be those who prefer to choose their cards one by one. Art galleries and museums are great places to find affordable postcards and the range will be broader and more diverse. Hunting out new and interesting cards can be a fun process in itself. With a surging interest in vintage accessories nowadays, old postcards can also be obtained from fairs and antique shops, adding a nostalgic and mysterious feel to an oracle reading.

A postcard oracle is something anyone can make because it doesn't require the creator to design the artwork on the cards. You simply choose the subjects you wish to use within your oracle, selecting them by which particular images move or inspire you. And there's always room for personalization: titles can be added by hand, and you can draw or paint into the images already there. There are many ink stamps and stencils to aid modification. This can, in some examples, help the deck to look more consistent and 'together' in terms of design.

What makes the postcard oracle attractive to those who use it is the ability to personalize their decks but also reassess them. You might start out with a humble 20 cards, but as time goes on, some may not feel as appropriate and new ones will be found along the way. The beauty of a deck like this is that it is fluid: cards that have served their use can be removed, and new ones can be added as and when. The deck can be as big as you wish, though decks with over 50 postcards might be more cumbersome and difficult to shuffle.

One thing that unites the cards of an oracle is the back design, and this can be an issue for some using a postcard oracle. The backs of postcards are pretty regular but, depending on the postcards you use, it might be easy to determine which is which from the reverse side. One way of disguising the backs is by covering them. Sticky-back plastic (sometimes known as Fablon) can be bought, and a couple of rolls should easily cover a deck of 60. Once stuck on and cut to size, a good corner-rounder (which can be bought in craft shops or online) will smooth off the sharp edges and make for a more comfortable shuffle.

Many of us have postcards stuffed away in old junk drawers or languishing in folders, often reminding us of times or people from our past. Using images of the places we have been to or cards from people we love — who, in some cases, may no longer be with us — can make for a very powerful and emotive tool. And if you're interested in designing your own oracle deck from scratch, putting together a postcard oracle can be a good way to experiment with deck structuring and customization!

USING ORIGINAL ARTWORK

Of course, many creators will want to create their own oracle from scratch. We've already gone over how you can tailor your images to convey your cards' meanings, and now we'll think about the different methods you can use to create those images.

DRAWING AND PAINTING

This might seem the most obvious way of creating a tarot or oracle deck, and the means of doing so are exhaustive. To date, tarots have been created in pen, ink, watercolors, acrylics, and oils, but the list of materials one can use is endless. Drawing and painting an oracle deck is a wonderful way to really put your spin on the cards. You can control the style and how each image conveys meaning. Are you going to be naturalistic or surrealist? How will you integrate symbolism? And what texture of paints or pencils will best evoke the feeling you want?

The obvious difference between these decks and those designed in the aforementioned mediums is the amount of time the project will take. Unless you already have a body of work you can repurpose (see 'Using pre-existing artwork'), the drawing or painting of a deck may be extremely time-consuming. With that in mind, it's important to keep up momentum. This is easier with an oracle deck (which can be any length) than with a tarot — as many optimistic artists have discovered, 78 cards are a lot of work! Not assessing how much time it will take beforehand might negatively impact the art: for some tarot decks, it is evident that an artist has invested more time and thought in the Major cards than the Minors. This can lead to a deck where some of the cards might appear rushed or not up to the same standard as others, which can be frustrating to the reader.

Because of the time involved with drawing or painting a deck, ask yourself: How long do you envisage the creative process to be? If one card will take six months to make, are you comfortable with your deck maybe taking years to complete? Many great oracle and tarot decks have taken up to a decade or more to create. However, before even putting down your first stroke, it is always worth considering how long each card will take you. We have all experienced starting something with gusto only to put it on the backburner when we realize it has become more work than we'd prepared for. While it can be satisfying to create something simply for the experience of creating it, if your goal is to produce a complete deck for future use, then you may want to establish a clear timeframe. That way, you can decide which medium to use so that you can complete your deck within that time.

There are other considerations when embarking on a project like this, such as visual consistency. The style of an artist will likely evolve over the time it takes to complete a project, and this can lead to cards looking disjointed or out of synch as a whole. It is not unusual for a designer, once finished, to redo or tweak earlier cards so that they fit together cohesively as a unit.

TESTING MATERIALS

Use this space to test out some of the different pencils, paints, oils etc. that you can use. What feeling does each one evoke? Which do you think best matches your theme?

With this in mind, consider the materials you intend to use before you begin. If you have decided, for example, to create a deck with shimmering bronze highlights, make sure that the chosen paint is readily available and, if you think it will be difficult to find your supplies a year down the track, stock up beforehand. This kind of forward-thinking will avoid disappointments later on, as switching materials during your project could result in noticeable differences between images when the deck is finished.

Rosario Salerno

Creator of *The New Choice Tarot de Marseille*

What inspired you to create The New Choice Tarot de Marseille?

I decided to create a tarot deck because I really liked the traditional Major Arcana and I thought it would be a good inspiration for my work. I had known about tarot for a long time and the archetypes and symbols really fascinated me. It began as more of an experiment for me, to see how it would look if I created the images myself, filtered by my own style. I wanted an excuse to draw a lot because, during that period, I was feeling stuck; I had wanted to immerse myself in something creative and had been used to drawing comic book characters, but I didn't always find the accompanying stories so easy to think up. Tarot already had its own story, which meant that there were lots of drawings to complete, each with their own narrative built in.

What challenges did you face?

At first, I was only going to create the Major Arcana. After the first three, I knew I could definitely make 22 — I was probably creating one a day. But then, after the first five or six, I decided to slow down. A friend of mine, who has read cards for a very long time, showed me a book by Jodorowsky. She told me that what I had created was beautiful but, if I was going to design the deck for real, that I needed to study the original *Tarot de Marseille*. What I had created so far was a mixture of different disciplines I had found online, so I began to study the symbolism of the *Marseille,* using Jodorowsky's book, and redesigned the first five. I chose that tradition because I found those in the *Rider-Waite-Smith* tarot to be sad and sometimes negative. I liked the flexibility of the *Marseille,* but I knew that I had to do my research properly. My knowledge of tarot was slim, and I didn't want for an expert to look at my work and for it to not make sense.

Did you consider any other medium when creating this deck?

It was very natural for me to draw and paint my first deck, even though making the tarot images as sculptures had been suggested to me already. I really wanted to see how they would look in my style of drawing because that is what I love to do. I have always been a comic geek, and spent my whole childhood watching anime, which is very popular in Italy. My parents would be working in their shop and I would be at home watching six episodes , one after the other, as I didn't have many friends and was quite lonely. Making my own

Roy de Deniers

characters and stories has always been my [favorite] thing to do, so I wanted to bring the antique figures in the *Marseille* to life. I would look at the characters, such as *La Papess*, and think about what she would do all day if she was a real person.

How did you make your Marseille individual?

On some days, I would make a card and then I would go out clubbing. I would see someone while I was out and I'd wonder how they might look as the sphinx from the *Wheel of Fortune*, as an example. I used some of the clothing I saw on my nights out to influence the costumes worn by the characters in the deck. Sometimes, I would use specific models. The direction of some of the poses in the *Marseille* are significant, and therefore complex, so I used live models for those.

Did you create your deck in isolation or did you seek feedback during the process?

It has been really important for me to see what people think. While designing my current deck, *New Voice Tarot*, it is rewarding and motivating to receive feedback after the hard work invested in each image. I think that my work is better for seeking opinion as I go along. People have really helped by sharing their knowledge, as I was not an expert when I started my first tarot. If I had not shown my friend in the first place, she never would have advised me to reconsider my approach. I still welcome personal opinion and feedback, which can sometimes be extremely beneficial, though I have a better understanding of the tarot these days.

What advice would you give to someone who is considering making their own tarot deck?

I would suggest that people consider why they would like to design one. Ego can become a big part of an artist's motivation, but I think it is important to remember that a tarot — if intended for sale — will be used by other people. I enjoy decks that focus on the light. Because we probably learn more from the shadows in life, I have tried to give the darker cards [in The New Voice Tarot] a positive spin.

Roy de Baton

XVI

La Maison Dieu

Page Right: *The New Choice Tarot de Marseille*, Salerno, R.

PHOTOGRAPHY

Because drawing and painting are the traditional modes of oracle illustration, this can be a hurdle if that's not your preferred medium. However, this is not the only way an oracle can be designed, even if you want to create the images from scratch yourself. While finding an artist to render the images is always a possibility, there are other means of creative expression available — and photography is just one of them.

These days, photography is accessible to just about anyone: all the budding photographer requires is a phone with a built-in camera, and they are ready to go. In this sense, almost everyone is capable of sharing their viewpoint or place in the world at the click of a few buttons. Even the most inexperienced but snap-happy photographer is one filter away from a professional-looking image due to the amount of photo editing apps available. This, of course, makes photography one of the most accessible methods of oracle creation.

Photography, in itself, can be as emotionally provocative as any painting, since it makes contact in a very real way with its subject. It can depict real tears or genuine laughter, capturing a moment in time forever. Who hasn't been magically transported back to how they once felt just by looking at a photograph from their past?

Deciding whether to use color (whether natural or overly saturated) or monochrome can drastically change the mood of a picture. For a deck intended to empower and encourage positive vibrations, it would make sense to include fresh and warm colors. In an oracle that is deeply reflective and concerned with the darker crevices of the psyche, photographs that exclude color may be more appropriate.

Photography is a popular medium for many deck creators, especially thanks to innovations like Photoshop and other professional editing programs. These allow you to edit your images, combining them with others or creating surreal effects. Considering the otherworldly nature of oracles, you can use photography as a basis for extensive editing, allowing you to incorporate symbolism and transport your reader to a world just a few steps away from reality.

That's not to say that more traditional, naturalistic photography can't be used for an oracle deck. There are many oracles that feature photographs of nature, slightly adjusted for both mood and printing purposes, including warm sunsets, flowers, and rushing water. In some cases, the camera is able to bring sacred images from the other side of the world into our homes and hands via a deck of oracle cards. In the world of tarot, photography has allowed many readers to explore places they might never visit in person, such as Paris, Prague, Haiti, and New York, since popular decks have been created around each.

Approaching an oracle through the lens of a photographer can help you discover the magic in the world around you. And this can also help you develop your deck, even if you choose a different medium for the final form.

PHOTO WALK

At an early point in the creation process, take your camera on a photo walk. This can be before or after you've set a theme. If before, then you can seek inspiration in the world around you: look for the magical in the everyday and perhaps you'll discover some scenes to include in your deck! If you've already set a theme, take at least 20 pictures that are related to it. Try not to be prescriptive — just capture whatever reminds you in some way of that theme. When you get back, sift through the images and you might find a natural pattern emerging that will help you structure your deck. These photos can form the basis of your oracle, or you can use them as a jumping-off point for creating the deck using a different medium.

Photography is a popular option for the modern deck designer, but it is not new. Perhaps the first photographic tarot is *The Mountain Dream Tarot* by Bea Nettles. The original deck now resides in The Cary Collection of Playing Cards, held at the Beinecke Rare Book and Manuscript Library of Yale University in the United States. It was published in 1975, though the idea came to Bea in a dream five years previously (hence the name).

What fascinates many about *The Mountain Dream Tarot* is that it was put together long before the existence of Photoshop. Whereas it is easy to search for symbolic imagery online these days (if you want a sword, Google Images will give you a plethora to choose from), all of the symbols, landscapes, and props that Bea needed had to be found in the real world. When Bea needed a boat for the ferryman in the *Six of Swords*, she had no other option than to find a ferry and rent it. Many of the costumes were recycled from old clothes or swathes of fabric; painted plates, in some cases, became *Pentacles*.

While many of us think of a prospective deck as being something we will eventually sell and distribute, the first copy of *The Mountain Dream Tarot* was a singular art piece in itself. It was printed onto photographic paper, which was placed between two pieces of frosted Mylar, and was then stitched around the edges to keep the layers together. The 1975 first edition, which is extremely rare and valuable nowadays, was limited to a 1,000 copies and Bea says: "after they'd gone, I thought that was it". However, with the birth of the internet, many found their way to the photographs online and a second edition was requested by fans.

Bea Nettles
Creator of *The Mountain Dream Tarot*

·⌒⦂⌒·

How did you become inspired to create The Mountain Dream Tarot?

When I was at graduate school in Illinois in the [spring] of 1970, somebody handed me a copy of *The Pictorial Key to the Tarot* by Edward Arthur Waite. There was one sculpture student who saw my work and said: "you would probably like this kind of stuff" and showed me her copy of the book. All I had, from that time onwards, were the little black and white line drawings within it to refer to and the short descriptions that went with each one fascinated me. There were a lot of portraits in my work at that time, and for some of the self-portraits I would go to thrift shops to find things to dress up in. After I graduated, I went to the Penland School in North Carolina for the summer and I had the book with me. So, while at school, I did one self-portrait of myself as the *Queen of Pentacles*, wearing this amazing black taffeta dress with stars on it that I'd found for 50 cents. I probably used a whole roll of film for that, which was just [12] shots.

I don't think I was consciously considering making a whole deck of [tarot] cards at that point but after shooting the *Queen of Pentacles*, I asked an instructor if he would pose for *The Magician*. And that is how it all started. I was lucky to have a lot of people around me, so some of the portraits were taken rather quickly.

What do you think photography adds to a deck that other mediums cannot?

Believability: that there is someone like the character in that card walking around. There were times when I would approach someone and ask them to model for me, kind of based on their looks, but I would soon find out that their energy was similar to the figure in said card and I hadn't known that. *The Devil,* as an example, was someone I was dating at that time who eventually ended up cheating on me. There were other timely events too. When I was printing the *Ten of Swords*, showing a man lying dead beneath ten swords, I'd just thrown the image into the fixer. A little girl from across the street knocked on the door and said: "Bea, did you know someone was just shot dead in your yard?" I'd not heard, because I'd been in the darkroom with the music on printing that exact card when someone walking across my yard was killed in some kind of gang retaliation, drive-by shooting.

It is important to remember that these are real people. I often thought about what would happen if this deck made its way out into the world and how it would affect [them] in years

XIV
Temperance

to come. I had people sign casual model releases but, considering those who posed for the pictures, I have resisted the deck being taken on by larger publishing houses as I never felt comfortable releasing it into the world in some massive print form.

Were there any difficulties you encountered while working on The Mountain Dream Tarot?

We started off with props that were not too complex; we gathered sticks and things that would look like Wands. But as we went along, it got more complicated, since some cards have elements like a lion or an eagle on them. As an example, for *Temperance*, which shows my sister, I knew she would need angel wings. She wore my dad's bathrobe backwards for the portrait and the wings were made from a hula skirt that my mother had been given after World War II. We tied it to her back and bunched it up a little and, later, I painted out parts of the skirt on the negative so that it would eventually look like wings. Most people, young people especially, cannot imagine a world without Photoshop or even digital cameras. This was all shot on 2¼ black and white film, which meant that each roll had to be processed and then I would have to composite the images together. There was a lot of crazy manipulation that had to be done, and I knew a lot of tricks in the darkroom because of my background in photography and painting.

The Tower was an interesting one. First of all, the tower itself was shot against a very bright sky, which meant that on the negative it was all black. The two figures in the image are both my brother-in-law. I took him over to the playground and had him hang from his knees on a jungle gym so I could literally photograph him upside-down and make it look as though he was falling. On the two negatives, I very carefully painted everything out except the figures, using black paint. To get the blast in the picture, I laid a sheet of glass over the photo paper and sprinkled cornmeal over it so that when the tower was exposed the cornmeal blocked the light and made it look like it was blowing up. After that, I put one figure into the enlarger, printed that and took it away; I then added the final figure. The process included three exposures to make the print and if I didn't get the figures where I wanted them, I'd have to start all over again. Some of the cards were even more involved than that.

It's important to remember that this project took five years. For me now, that is nothing, since I will spend ten years on a body of work, but it was a big commitment back then. Even the process of putting them together took time. After ordering the boxes, I added all of the labels. Actually, I cut the cards too, from the big press sheets with a guillotine cutter — which was quite time consuming — and then I collated them. I had a machine that would round the corners, which I would do one card at a time. It involved a lot of working by hand and was a big commitment.

What did you enjoy about the process?

Making the deck was an adventure. There was delayed gratification from doing it in the way I did, but I think that is important. At times it was a scavenger hunt — having to go to a natural history museum, for example, to find a stuffed eagle and bull; it all took time and wasn't instant. I might start to sound old now but many people these days expect things to happen so quickly and, for that reason, they don't treasure stuff as much. I didn't have much money and there was no funding for the project, so I had to be resourceful.

If someone wanted to create a photographic tarot, what advice would you give them?

These days, I would say that you'd probably want to learn something like Photoshop since not many people have darkrooms. In terms of putting a deck together, this would be a valid tool. If you just want one deck for yourself, then there are great places, such as Printers Studio, who will print two or three copies. The unit cost usually goes down the more that you order. I am a gardener and I create my own plant identification manuals; nobody ever sees them other than me but that is the great thing about print-on-demand — if you want a physical deck of your own creation, it is possible. There is no upfront investment other than your time; whereas with the offset decks, you have to make at least a thousand to get the press going.

In modern times, the method of creating the photographic deck may have changed since *The Mountain Dream Tarot*, but photographers are no less resourceful or creative. In fact, many comparisons can be made. The artist Dita Von Queef decided to combine her drag work with the tarot's Major Arcana and Carl Jung's theory of the archetypes. She says: "I wanted to transform myself into the various archetypes depicted in the Major Arcana, but to embody them in a way that was an authentic expression of me as a queer female artist. The aim was to create a strong visual character that maintained the ability to be interpreted in a variety of ways, depending on the viewer."

What is comparable about the work of both Bea Nettles and Dita Von Queef is their resourcefulness. Von Queef, due to the 2020 lockdown in Melbourne, Australia, could only use what was accessible in her home to inspire her — but she enjoyed the challenge of having to create costumes using unconventional materials. It kept her busy and in a constant state of play with her environment. "I created a makeshift photo studio in my bathroom! I live alone so it was a process of setting up, dressing up and then pressing record. I later screen-grabbed the best images and digitally altered them. The whole thing was a one-woman show!"

COLLAGE

Collage can be one of the most magical ways of creating an image. While the putting together of different pieces of paper can be a meditative practice — allowing the artist to step out of their physical landscape and into their inner world — just a slight change of position or a new component in a picture can alter a card design in ways we might never have expected.

In this sense, collage connects you to the creative and intuitive side of the brain because, often, the best pieces are not those that have been overthought and over-planned but those with which we allow our soul or a higher vibration to guide us.

THE LOVERS

THE WORLD.

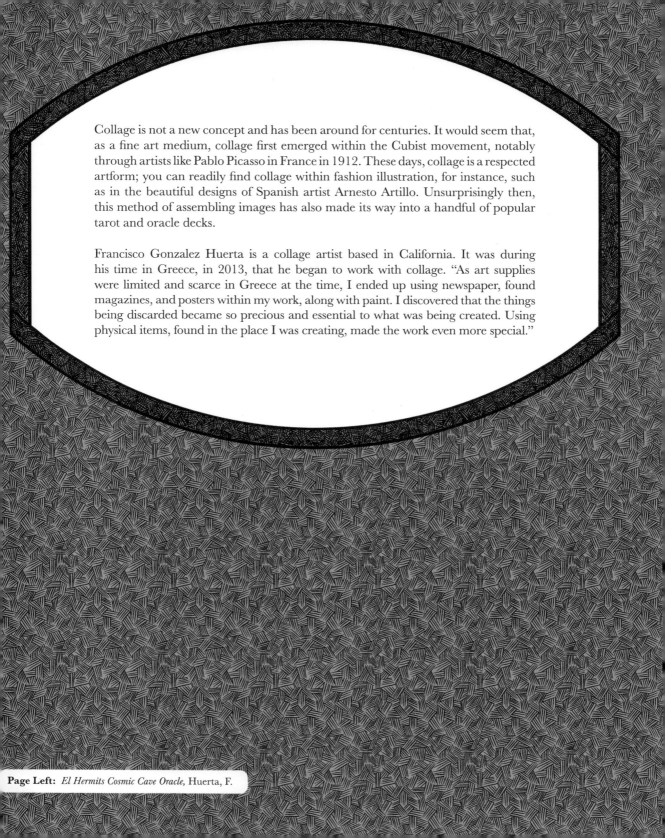

Collage is not a new concept and has been around for centuries. It would seem that, as a fine art medium, collage first emerged within the Cubist movement, notably through artists like Pablo Picasso in France in 1912. These days, collage is a respected artform; you can readily find collage within fashion illustration, for instance, such as in the beautiful designs of Spanish artist Arnesto Artillo. Unsurprisingly then, this method of assembling images has also made its way into a handful of popular tarot and oracle decks.

Francisco Gonzalez Huerta is a collage artist based in California. It was during his time in Greece, in 2013, that he began to work with collage. "As art supplies were limited and scarce in Greece at the time, I ended up using newspaper, found magazines, and posters within my work, along with paint. I discovered that the things being discarded became so precious and essential to what was being created. Using physical items, found in the place I was creating, made the work even more special."

Page Left: *El Hermits Cosmic Cave Oracle,* Huerta, F.

In collage, Francisco found a way of better expressing his emotions. "If I feel frustrated, I might crumple a piece of paper and add it to the collage. If I feel sensitive, I'll be extremely careful about how I cut something from a magazine. If I feel a need to burn a piece of paper and add it to the work, I will do that. Collage embodies the physical world."

The process of collage can be never-ending and many collage artists will consistently collect images, storing them away for just the right time. Like others, Francisco has his valued paper piles which he can sort through when he has an idea or flash of inspiration. "Once I have finished searching," he says, "I will clear everything around me and see what I am left with. One of my art professors once reminded me that 'less is more'. Work does not need to be over-the-top to trigger a reaction and, for that reason, I usually know when an image is done and not to overwork it. All objects already have a vast amount of symbolism within them, and when you have too much occurring in one place it can be overwhelming."

Many collage artists enjoy the spontaneity of the medium: not knowing what will be created until it comes together can be exciting and inspiring. Some elements may be harder to locate but, when found, are rewarding and increase motivation. Of course, as Francisco reminds us, not everything goes right the first time. "There have been pieces that have ended up a disaster. These works usually end up in the reuse pile and are recycled." Collaging is an ongoing process, meaning that just because a specific piece does not work well for one idea, if stored away, it can become invaluable at a later date for another.

What is appealing to many deck creators is that found items can assist in conveying mood, whether that is through texture, color, pattern, or the time and place of their origin. For anyone working on a themed deck, collage can directly arouse feelings and memories within a viewer. This can also be a good starting point for creation. Try collecting items that remind you of your theme — think, if you will, of a vintage-style deck created with old bus tickets, copies of handwritten letters, or antique photography.

Page Right: *El Hermits Cosmic Cave Oracle,* Huerta, F.

Megan Skinner
Creator of *The Couture Tarot*

What was your reason for creating a deck?

The inspiration for my deck was my mother. She gave me my first tarot deck when I was a teenager. I began to create my deck, *The Couture Tarot*, when she was terminally ill. I was filled with grief and needed a way to channel it, so I began to create some tarot art. I started with one card, and then another, until finally I had a whole deck. My mother was a seamstress, and when I was young, we spent many happy hours together going through fashion magazines as she would recreate some of the outfits for me. *The Couture Tarot* was created through collage art using fashion magazines. I like to think that I became a mystical seamstress, cutting and sewing (or, in this case, pasting) different images together to create individual tarot tapestries. I had always wanted to create my own deck, but never had the courage. When my mother was passing, I thought: "Life is short, so if not now, then when?"

Why did you choose collage as a medium for designing your deck?

I had the Taschen book about Da Vinci, which is one of those vast books, the size of a bible. I also had a I always enjoyed doing collage art, so using it was a natural fit when I decided to create my own deck. The cards of *The Couture Tarot* are collages made from images in fashion magazines. To me, high fashion is art, and is one of my greatest inspirations.

What is the advantage of creating a deck with collage?

I think that collage art is greatly underrated, and some believe that collage artists are not 'real' artists. It takes vision and skill to make meaningful collage. I liken it to an alchemical process, as one combines different ingredients (images) together to create a whole new substance and vision. The alchemy comes from how the images are put together in a divine synthesis.

Emperor IV

Hermit IX

Ten of Pentacles

What were the benefits of creating your own deck?

The thrill of putting your own stamp and vision on the cards of the tarot is priceless! In the best sense, creating your own deck is a magical adventure: one that can open doors to new sources of inspiration, and a deeper [knowledge] of the cards you're creating. In doing so, your relationship with tarot will be transformed in profound ways. Committing to creating a whole deck is embarking on a spiritual process, and no matter the outcome, you will benefit from the journey.

What drawbacks did you encounter?

The biggest drawback in creating a deck for me was, honestly, money. Once your deck is finished, there can be the cost of producing it: printing fees and, in my case, hiring a graphic designer to put my artwork into a usable format. This can be expensive. I think that most who create our own decks want them to be available and out in the world, so there's also marketing costs. There are those who successfully launch their decks, and I hope to be one, but know that it may be more a labor of love than a source of income. Is it worth it though? Absolutely!

What advice would you give to anyone creating a deck of their own?

Trust your inspiration! If you feel called to create your own deck — and I do believe it is a calling — trust that you have something unique and special to offer. One of the beauties of tarot is that its images and archetypes are open to interpretation and new and different versions are a part of keeping its wisdom vital and applicable to current times.

Three of Cups

Nine of Cups

Nine of Swords

STEP-BY-STEP COLLAGE

1. The first step in creating a collage is to collect media for use. Magazines are an obvious choice, but don't feel that you need to go out and buy a handful of expensive fashion journals. Brochures and catalogues can be found for free and charity shops are a perfect option for finding old books and other material cheaply. Most home printers include scanners, so if you wish to use a picture from a favorite book but don't want to ruin it, this is a good way of duplicating the image for collage.

2. Collage should arouse your intuition, so it is a good idea to start looking through your chosen materials when you are in a calm state of mind and can dedicate a few hours to the process. Thumb your way through the pages, allowing your eye to select anything of interest. Don't overthink at this point or allow the articles surrounding the images to influence your decision. If a picture grabs you, for whatever reason, rip it out. Once you have a pile of images, you are ready to start work.

3. If you intend to replicate this deck through printing, it might be useful to research which dimensions will fit snugly onto a card without your design being cropped. Also check to make sure that these dimensions fit whatever scanner you intend to use. This is helpful if your collages will be bigger than the average oracle card. If you have decided to use the collages themselves as the finished deck, then you could use pre-cut card stock as a canvas for your collages. Corner rounders, for a professional effect, are also reasonably priced.

4. Using a viewfinder can be a useful trick when working with collage. A card frame, with the center cut out to the exact size of your card, can be helpful when you wish to see whether a design works or not. It enables the artist to eliminate the visual clutter and see how the final image will look before cutting and pasting.

5. Separate out images into different piles. Some will work better as backgrounds, while you may be inclined to use others for the foreground. Let the images dictate what goes where, moving things around to see if the components speak in a different way when reassembled. Adding and eliminating pieces is all part of the process, so allow yourself time to experiment and play.

6. While collage works well as an intuitive process, consciously looking for images will be necessary for some designers. If you are creating a tarot, for example, it will be relevant to honor the traditional meanings, symbolism, and titles. While your Devil card, sometimes representing temptation in a reading, might not show a horned figure, you may want to keep your eyes open for images that you find tempting — a chocolate cake, perhaps, or something traditional that most readers would find tempting.

7. Once you feel as though an image is done — and you'll know when that is — it is time to put the piece together. You might want to take a quick photo for reference, just in case the ordering and layering is disrupted as you begin to assemble it. There are many kinds of glue available so it might make sense to try out a few beforehand. A quality glue stick is a practical option, and some sprays (though more expensive) can allow for you to adjust and reapply while you are pasting the images down.

8. If you intend to make just the one deck for yourself, then thinking about how to back the cards is your next concern. Cards can be backed with adhesive backing paper, of which you'll find many designs available, and if you are wishing to protect the fronts (and stop pieces of your collage ripping or unsticking), a heated laminator should do the trick.

Try it here :

DIGITAL ILLUSTRATION

While there will always be those who prefer the hands-on approach of physically assembling a collage or literally putting pen to paper, the number of decks created using computer design programs has skyrocketed since the turn of the 21st Century.

Advances in image manipulation programs have allowed many designers to create their own imagery at the click of a mouse. Recently, simplicity has become a trend of its own. You can now produce flat and consistently colored images with software such as Adobe Illustrator, achieving minimalistic, clean, contemporary artwork. Many modern tarots and oracles are created in this way.

With programs such as Procreate, you can draw straight onto a tablet, making it easier to digitally illustrate on-the-go. Offering a variety of different options, from charcoal to oil paint, the Apple Pen (used with versions of the iPad) can mimic most art techniques with its large selection of 'brushes'. Aside from the outlay for some of these products, the ever-growing, adapting nature of software allows for less accumulation of materials in the long run, greater convenience and the ability to correct any mistakes without a fuss.

Probably the most revolutionary development within design technology has been Photoshop, which has given artists the opportunity to manipulate and integrate photography at the touch of a button. Even the novice can effectively create something interesting, though a better working knowledge of the software will garner greater and more sophisticated results. This can help you achieve effects that would be challenging in traditional illustration, adding light, different backgrounds, distortions, or surreal manipulations to really convey the meaning of your card.

While those with little experience may struggle to begin with, there is always help at hand and there are many guides available. But these days, most of us are just one click away from YouTube, where literally hundreds of free online tutorials exist and are consistently being made. Photoshop has become the industry standard, and it is often included in art education courses. It is evident in some decks that images have been digitally enhanced or constructed, but most artists will benefit from this kind of program, regardless of their artistic medium. When photographed, paintings and drawings can sometimes look lacklustre or dull, so a boost of brightness or contrast could be what is needed to give an image vitality and conviction. Photoshop also allows for the removal of any scratches or flaws that might have occurred during painting.

39

STRAWBERRY

Yasmeen Westwood
Creator of *The Tarot of Enchanted Dreams*

How did The Tarot of Enchanted Dreams come to be?

I hadn't intended to create a tarot deck, but after I had my son I suffered from severe postnatal depression. I am a very private person and find it difficult to share my feelings with others, so it was hard to explain what I was experiencing. I tried face-to-face [counseling] but I felt I was only telling the [counselor] what she wanted to hear. During this time, I continued to have this same vision: it was of a heart, full of flowers, but it was bleeding. I knew that it was significant and that I had to create the image but because I couldn't draw, I wasn't quite sure how. However, I knew the basics of Photoshop. I ended up going onto YouTube and looking at tutorials about photo-manipulation.

I went on to create the image of the flowers, which became the *Three of Swords* in my deck. It mirrored how I was feeling at that time: totally lost and grieving for the 'me' that I felt didn't exist anymore. From then on, as I created more images, I [realized] I could express how I was feeling through my art. It became very therapeutic, more so than if I was talking to someone. As I continued to create them, I [realized] how much they resembled the cards of a tarot deck. I decided to try to make all the cards and would design, to begin with, when I was feeling down. I made all of the *Swords* cards when I was at my lowest. Bit by bit, in four months, the deck was complete.

Did you intend for the deck to be published?

No. It had started as something that assisted me during a difficult time in my life but, as time went on, I started to get a good feeling about it and where it might end up. People around me couldn't understand why I was doing it, since they advised that I didn't know anything about art, but I continued all the same, feeling driven and directed by a higher power. It was almost as if I [channeled] the ideas and messages, which in turn became my therapy. I could sit for hours and hours just doing this and not think for a second about being depressed. It took me into a different world, which allowed me to see beauty that I was failing to appreciate elsewhere in life.

What is your process of creating a deck?

If I am creating a deck for myself and am writing the booklet, like with *The Tarot of Enchanted Dreams*, I usually have a good idea of how I want something to look. I'll go on a hunt for imagery that might suit, starting with my own stock folder that I keep on my computer. This contains many sub-folders such as *male, female, furniture, space, flowers,* and *nature*. If I can, I will build a card around what I have already got because I know that I'm using images that the artist has already approved. If I want to design a *Queen of Cups,* for instance, I will search through my files for the right woman to begin with and then see what else I have to build the image. If there is something specific that I don't have, I will begin to look through the online stock galleries. I have a list of preferred people I like to use, so I usually check them out first. Using the same sources also means that the artwork remains consistent throughout the deck.

From then on, I take things into Photoshop and start playing around with the different elements. For example, in *The Magician* from the deck I am currently working on, I had to change the hand to hold Mercury. The original figure had his hands in his pockets, so I found another image that had the [correct] hand posture. The jacket in the image was brown and plain, so I found stars and moons to add to it and changed the [color].

There are some free downloadable add-ons for Photoshop called Photoshop Actions and these allow you, once the digital collaging and manipulations have been done, to give something an overall style. I always use Paint Action to give it the look of a painting, complete with brushstrokes. I will usually adjust the opacity of the filter, though, so that it looks more convincing. Once finished, I always add a canvas texture over the top of it so that it looks like a piece of artwork.

What difficulties arose when you were creating your deck?

Finding the right image was not always easy, and searching was very time-consuming. I am a bit of a perfectionist and don't like to compromise, so finding the ideal picture could take many hours. I don't think people always factor in how long something like this will take within the process. There would be instances where I would be searching for the perfect hair for someone, since I added the hair to a lot of the figures afterwards, and it would take days for me to find just the right kind that flowed in the way I wanted it to.

Time is also something worth considering if you are a Photoshop novice, because learning how to do things can take up more time than you'd expect. As I was creating my first deck, I was watching tutorials — finding out how to cut the images out, for example — and learning different and vital techniques. Actually, finding time to do all of this, especially if you have another job or a full calendar, can be difficult.

What was the benefit of creating this deck?

One of the most significant benefits is that it pushed me into what I do now. If I'd not experienced the postnatal depression, I'd never have known that I was capable of creating this work; something so beautiful came from something so dark and I [realized] that this is what I was supposed to be doing my whole life. It's funny because when I was about [14] years old, in school, I'd wanted to take Art as a subject, but I'd been told that "Muslim girls don't do art," and was asked what point there would be in my choosing it. However, my interest in drawing and images continued to flourish. The postnatal depression pushed me into doing something about it. It was as though a voice had said: "This is your time to do what you always wanted to do and what you should be doing."

The highlight for me was seeing the finished project, whether that was the completed deck published, or just a finished image at the end of the day. It was rewarding to look at something and think 'I can't believe that I created that!'.

What advice would you give to someone wishing to create a tarot or oracle deck?

I would remind someone about how much time making it takes and to not believe that it is something that can be created overnight. You have to be really dedicated if you want to get it done. If you are creating something digitally, as I have, a lot of your time will be spent researching and looking for the right components. For those reasons, you have to be prepared to really put in the time and effort to do it properly. Aside from that, I would suggest that the person enjoys the process and [lets] it evolve in its own time, since these things cannot be rushed.

For anyone who thinks they cannot create a deck because they cannot draw, I'd suggest that they think again. I cannot draw to save my life, but I have created a handful of decks, some yet to be published. There are loads of different ways of creating art, so don't get hung up on just the one. If you know how to turn on a computer and search for a picture, there are so many tutorials on YouTube to assist you with taking an image and turning it into a collage. Some may still argue that this method of creating is not art, but I disagree: how you compose the imagery makes it your own and that *is* an art.

INDIVIDUAL TECHNIQUES

Creating a deck of cards can often be a cathartic experience — one in which the creator finds out as much about themselves as they do about the subject they are exploring or the tool they are designing. Within this creative process, new ideas can develop quite naturally. In my own experience with collage, adding paint and embellishing images with marker pens and gold detailing enhanced what was already on the page, lifting specific aspects and highlighting elements of symbolism. You might experience what I would call 'happy accidents', where something does not necessarily go to plan but produces a new and unexpected way of working that is satisfying.

So, while you're creating your oracle, open yourself up to the possibilities. Try deliberately using a tool the wrong way — like painting with the handle rather than the brush — or pay attention to what is created when you accidentally apply the wrong effect in Photoshop. Sometimes it's only by breaking the mold that we can discover new ways of creating — and these can open doors we never knew were originally closed to us.

This was the case for Deborah Koff-Chapin who released her SoulCards oracle deck 25 years ago. When remembering how her journey into what is now referred to as 'touch drawing' began, she says: "On my last day in art school in 1974, I had a creative awakening. In a moment of playful exploration, I moved my fingertips on a paper towel that was intended to wipe an inked plate. Lifting the towel, I saw childlike scrawls that had appeared on the underside from the pressure of my touch. I laughed ecstatically with this discovery! This was a direct mode of expression that fulfilled my longing for a more natural way to draw." Diving into this mode of creation, Deborah ended up creating not one but two decks using this technique — and she has sold over 70,000 copies in the US and Canada alone.

Deborah Koff-Chapin
Creator of *Soul Cards*

What was the most exciting part of the oracle-creating experience?

I was most excited by how the images have come alive in people's psyches since publishing. As an artist, I chose an alternative path to showing in art galleries; they seemed to cater to a limited and esoteric audience. My calling was to express and speak to something more universally human. In the form of *Soul Cards*, I have found the most direct and accessible way to share my art. My images have been finding their way around the world and into the hands of people since 1995. I keep hearing stories of the deep, intimate relationship people have with them. I have done very little to promote them since the original launch, yet they live on through word of mouth.

'Touch drawing' is a fresh and exciting way of creating images. How important is it for an oracle deck to stand out from the crowd?

There are so many decks on the market now, so standing out in some way seems essential. But it is a fine line to walk. The effort to make something unique does not necessarily bring forth an authentic and powerful creation.

Many mass-market decks seem to be based on writing, with illustrators hired to pictorialize the concepts. They can overlap in style and substance, becoming hard to differentiate. The indie movement has spawned more unique decks, often focusing on niche themes. Generally speaking, they seem to emerge from a deeper dedication on behalf of the creator. I guess dedication and authenticity are foundational, whether indie or [traditionally] published. A deck resonates with the core impulse from which it was created. If it wasn't created from a core impulse, it is another piece of merchandise or an illustration of concepts.

What led you to publish your deck?

I was lightly exploring the idea of doing a card deck. I had recently made small photographic prints of about 150 'touch drawings' but had shown them to nobody. At the time, I was working with a theatre group that performed stories from the audience. I would be on stage and create a large 'touch drawing' of the story while they enacted it. Before leaving for the airport on my way to a performance, I had thrown the pile of photos into my purse. On the plane, I sat next to Will McGreal, a new member of the group. Acting on impulse, I pulled the photos out of my purse, saying: "You may be interested in these." His jaw dropped and he said: "This is what I've been looking for." It just so happened that he was a

tarot card reader. He had just given his own deck away that day, thinking he was not going to do readings anymore. I gave him the photos to take home, asking him to let me know if they worked as a deck.

One year, and twelve hundred readings later, he was continually repeating to me: "You've got to do the deck. Just do the deck." Using the images, his readings had completely changed. With tarot, his clients would wait passively for his interpretation. With these images, they were having a direct and emotional response. They were taking an active part in the readings, tapping into a wisdom and insight within [themselves] that they hadn't known they were capable of.

What is the benefit of creating cards without titles or accompanying interpretations in the guidebook?

I knew this was a risk when I first published the cards in 1995. But the energies around the deck were so strong that I trusted it would work. It was the only authentic approach for me. Some people begin with a body of written knowledge that they put into the form of a deck. Cards are then selected to illustrate the concept and direct the user to the written wisdom. For me, the images are the wisdom. If I were to write meanings, they would be my personal interpretation.

The power of *SoulCards* is that they provoke the user into looking more deeply and [trusting] their own inner wisdom. I love when someone sees an image in an entirely different way to how I do. The fact that the images were created from a non-verbal level enables people to engage with them on a non-verbal level, therefore making a bridge to their verbal mind through writing or talking about what they see. There is a guidebook [for the deck]; it provides ideas about ways to interact with the images through creative processes. I think of it as a 'mini-expressive arts manual'.

What advice would you give to someone who intends to create an oracle deck?

There are so many stages in bringing a deck into being. It takes much more than creating the art and writing. You have to be willing to care for your baby through all stages of production and then tend its life in the world. There are things you have to be willing to do that might not be in your nature as a creative, philosophical person: marketing, database development, bookkeeping and inventory, social media fulfillment. You can hire help but that creates higher overheads. It takes an all-out dedication to do whatever needs to be done.

Page Left: *The Soul Cards*, Koff-Chapin, D.

COLLABORATIONS AND COMMUNITY DECKS

Another way in which a deck can be created is through group collaboration. There are many decks on the market that are the work of more than one artist. Many are tied together by a theme, but not all. Having more than one artist working on a deck is a sure way of creating it more quickly and will also mean that there is a wider vision than from just one individual alone. Some decks have combined two or three artists, but there are others which have utilized someone different for every single card.

So, if you're interested in creating an oracle but you're not sure if you can fulfill all parts of the process yourself, why not reach out for a co-author? This can be someone who assists on any part of the process, or someone who has a particular strength in an area that you're unsure of. It can help to enlist your friends — you might be surprised who among your contacts has already been thinking of creating something like this.

You could even form a group around this purpose, with the deck being the finished project of many authors. That way, you can play around with different methods of creation. Why not create a mixed-media deck which reflects everyone's talents? The narrative that arises from such a community-focused deck would be rich and diverse; just as oracle decks are supposed to reflect life in order to divine meaning, so this kind of deck would provide a broad range of experiences on which to draw.

COMPANION BOOKS

Most oracle and tarot decks come with instructions, describing the meanings of the cards and how to use them. The nature of these companion books has changed a lot over the last 30 years. Decks that are now considered vintage would be packaged with a card-sized foldout sheet of definitions and — if you were lucky — might also include an example spread with them. As the years went by, this pamphlet morphed into what is now affectionately termed the 'little white book' by those in global tarot and oracle communities. The little white book (or LWB) varies from deck to deck. In some, you'll find a short introduction or biography of the creator, along with a few words or sentences for each card and a spread; many readers will choose to disregard the more minimal of these. However, not all of these small books are as vague. Some creators will go to a lot of trouble to include a significant amount of information about their deck in a short amount of space and these books, though small, can contain a wealth of insight.

In terms of packaging, much has altered in the world of card divination during just the last 10 years. Those who have taken the option to self-publish (and therefore have total control over their product) have produced some truly impressive examples of lavish presentation, causing even the big publishing houses to sit up and take notice. Schiffer Publishing, based in Pennsylvania, were probably the first to really take the experience of the consumer into account and consider how a deck of cards is presented; it might seem commonplace to receive gilded cards in a sturdy box with a magnetic clasp, but this was not always the way.

The 'little white book' also received a makeover. What were once foldaway (and throwaway) pamphlets have widely been transformed into meatier and more useful guidebooks: sometimes in color, with small images and full instructions. It is generally expected that if you produce a deck of cards, some kind of literature will be produced to go along with it. In fact, some deck collectors choose to rely entirely on these companion books for their tarot study, rather than opting to buy individually published tarot guides.

PAGES FROM THE "MYSTICAL MEDLEYS" BOOKLET

INTRODUCTION

LIKE SO MANY GOOD STORIES, IT ALL STARTED WITH THE DEVIL!

I'VE ALWAYS BEEN FASCINATED BY MAGICK, THE OCCULT, AND THE IMAGERY OF THE TAROT. I OWN SEVERAL DECKS, FROM FULLY USABLE TRADITIONAL ONES TO MORE MODERN ARTISTIC ONES, AND HAVE ALWAYS DREAMED OF CREATING MY OWN IN SOME WAY.

ONE OF MY OTHER BIG PASSIONS IS ANIMATION. I STUDIED ANIMATION AT UNIVERSITY AND IN MY LONG, VARIED ART CAREER I'VE OFTEN WORKED AS AN ANIMATOR. ONE PARTICULAR PROJECT WAS ACTUALLY WITH THE MIGHTY DISNEY COMPANY ITSELF... BUT THAT'S A STORY FOR ANOTHER DAY!

I'M FOND OF MANY ERAS OF ANIMATION, BUT PARTICULARLY THE VINTAGE RUBBER HOSE CARTOONS OF THE 1920S AND 30S. I'VE BEEN DRAWING MY OWN OCCULT AND GOTHIC CARTOON CHARACTERS IN THIS STYLE FOR A LONG TIME, SO IT SEEMED TO BE FATE THAT ONE DAY THE TWO WORLDS WOULD COME TOGETHER, AND THIS DECK WOULD FINALLY BE REALISED.

I KNEW I DIDN'T JUST WANT TO MAKE AN AESTHETIC, GOOD-LOOKING DECK THAT WAS ALL STYLE AND NO SUBSTANCE. I WANTED IT TO BE VEILED — IN THE TRUE, DEEPER MEANING OF TRADITIONAL TAROT — WHILE PAYING HOMAGE TO VINTAGE CARTOONS AND ALL OF THEIR WONDERFUL, INTRICATE SYMBOLISM.

BUT BACK TO THE MATTER IN HAND: THE DEVIL CARD IS WHERE I BEGAN. BEING SOMEONE WHO IS NATURALLY DRAWN TO THE DARK SIDE OF ANYTHING (I ALWAYS ROOT FOR THE BAD GUY IN MOVIES OR BOOKS AND HEAVY METAL IS MY GO-TO MUSIC), I THOUGHT, IF I COULD CAPTURE THAT CUTE, VINTAGE LOOK OF CLASSIC CARTOONS WITH THE MOST INFAMOUS OCCULT CARD, THEN I MAY WELL BE ONTO SOMETHING. SO I GAVE IT MY BEST SHOT... AND THE RESPONSE WAS AMAZING!

MY VERSION OF THE DEVIL WAS WELL RECEIVED, AND I WAS LUCKY ENOUGH TO GARNER THE INTEREST OF THE TAROT COMMUNITY AND ULTIMATELY THE ATTENTION OF DARREN AND KAY FROM LIMINAL II. THANKS TO THEIR ENCOURAGEMENT, HERE WE ARE TODAY — WITH MY MAGNUM OPUS IN YOUR HANDS.

I WANT TO PERSONALLY THANK YOU, THE PERSON READING THIS, FOR CHOOSING THIS DECK AND I HOPE YOU GET AS MUCH ENJOYMENT FROM IT AS I DID FROM CREATING IT.

BLESSED BE.

GARY HALL

6   7

Introduction and foreword

Details of the majors

0   I

THE FOOL

THE MORNING IS FULL OF JOY AS THE CAREFREE FOOL SETS OFF ON HIS JOURNEY, ALL POTENTIAL AND ENDLESS POSSIBILITIES, HIS HOPES AND DREAMS PACKED FOR THE TRIP WITH ONLY ONE EYE ON THE ROAD. DOES HE SEE WHERE THIS PATH IS LEADING HIM? IS HE LISTENING TO THE CALLS, WARNING OF DANGER AHEAD? OR IS HE CONFIDENT THAT HIS FEET WILL TAKE HIM EXACTLY WHERE HE WANTS TO GO, BLIND FAITH LEADING THE WAY?

ALL ADVENTURES BEGIN WITH A SINGLE STEP; DON'T BE AFRAID TO KNOW YOU KNOW NOTHING. THERE ARE CHOICES TO BE MADE AND EVERY CHOICE IS VALID. MUSTER YOUR STRENGTH, LISTEN TO YOUR HEART AND LET THE STORY BEGIN!

THE MAGICIAN

HEY PRESTO! TAKE CENTRE STAGE, FOR YOU ARE THE MIGHTY MYSTICAL MAGICIAN AND YOU CAN PERFORM MARVELOUS MIRACLES OF WONDER. ALL THINGS ARE POSSIBLE. USE THE TOOLS AVAILABLE TO YOU AND LET YOURSELF BECOME ONE WITH THE INFINITE UNIVERSE OF CREATION. HAPPINESS AND SUCCESS ARE GAINED FROM HARD WORK AND THE COMPLETION OF THE TASKS LIFE PLACES IN FRONT OF YOU; CHART YOUR OWN PATH AND LET YOUR MIND BE CARRIED AWAY TO IMAGINARY LANDS FULL OF AMAZING INVENTIONS.

YOUR IDEAS ARE YOUR UNIQUE SEEDS: THEY ONLY EXIST WITHIN YOU AND YOUR WONDERFUL WORLD. EXPAND YOUR HORIZONS, GROW THE FANCIFUL FLOWERS OF YOUR SPIRITUAL GARDEN, LET LOVE DIRECT YOUR WILL AND USE YOUR IMAGINATION TO CREATE NOT JUST GOOD THINGS BUT GREAT THINGS! ABRACADABRA!

10   11

CUPS

ACE OF CUPS: IT'S THE START OF A NEW LIFE. SOMETHING WONDERFUL HAS BEGUN, AND THIS CHEERFUL CLEANSING CUP IS YOUR VESSEL. KEEP IT EVER FLOWING WITH POSITIVITY AND JOY; FIND A BALANCE AND HARMONY THAT FILLS YOUR SOUL.

TWO OF CUPS: THERE'S TWO OF YOU (OR THERE WILL BE), BUT THERE ARE SOME MIGHTY EMOTIONS CIRCLING THAT NEED TO BE GRASPED. CONFLICTING OR COMPLEMENTARY, THEY MUST BE ADDRESSED TO BRING HARMONY AND BALANCE TO THIS RELATIONSHIP?

THREE OF CUPS: RAISE THOSE CUPS TO THE SKY AND DANCE THE DAY AWAY! CELEBRATE THE JOY YOU HAVE WON, GRAB YOUR FRIENDS AND MAKE A FUN-FILLED FIESTA OUT OF THE DAILY ROUTINE. THIS FROLICKING FESTIVITY IS A MAGICAL FEELING.

FOUR OF CUPS: WHAT'S UP BUTTERCUP? LIFE GOT YOU DOWN? SOMETIMES IT'S BEST TO TAKE A BREAK FROM ALL YOUR WORRIES AND WOES, BUT DON'T DWELL ON YOUR DISAPPOINTMENTS FOR TOO LONG. SAY YES TO THAT FRIENDLY OFFERING OF SUPPORT, THEY'VE GOT YOUR BACK.

FIVE OF CUPS: ARE YOU TOO OBSESSED WITH THE BLACKNESS OF YOUR OWN DESPAIR TO SEE THE WORLD AROUND YOU? IT MAY LOOK LIKE YOU CAN'T MOVE FORWARD RIGHT NOW, BUT TIME, LIKE THE RIVER, KEEPS FLOWING ONWARDS. CHOOSE THE CUPS FILLED WITH LOVE AND LEAVE THE REST BEHIND.

SIX OF CUPS: YOU'RE FEELING NICELY NOSTALGIC... IS THERE SOMETHING FROM YOUR CHILDHOOD YOU WANT TO TAKE A CLOSER LOOK AT? AS AN ADULT LOOKING BACK TO THOSE HALCYON DAYS YOU CAN USE THESE FEELINGS OF CHILDLIKE FANTASY AND LOVE TO BUILD A BETTER FUTURE AND EXPAND YOUR HORIZONS.

SEVEN OF CUPS: A CABINET OF CURIOSITIES, A WORLD OF WHIMS AND WONDROUS WEALTH. ALL OF THIS STANDS BEFORE YOU AND IT CAN ALL BE YOURS. TAKE YOUR TIME AND CHOOSE WISELY. USE YOUR IMAGINATION AND CREATIVITY TO THE FULLEST, BUT DON'T GET CAUGHT WITH YOUR HEAD IN THE CLOUDS!

40   41

Details of the minors

Spreads specialised to the deck

LIGHTS! CAMERA! ACTION!

5   4

1

3

2

LIFE IS A MOVIE, BABY, AND YOU'RE THE STAR! THIS SPREAD TREATS YOUR LIFE AS THOUGH YOU'RE PLAYING THE LEAD ROLE — BUT YOU'RE AN ACTOR, AND FAME CAN BE CRUEL.

CARD 1 REPRESENTS YOU, AND THE ROLE YOU WILL PLAY ON LIFE'S GREAT STAGE. CARD 2, THE DIRECTOR, IS SOMEONE WHO WILL HELP GUIDE YOU ALONG THE WAY. IS THIS SOMEONE YOU RECOGNISE, OR SOMEONE YOU HAVEN'T MET YET? CARD 3 IS YOUR SCRIPT, SOMETHING TO REFER BACK TO WHEN YOU CAN'T QUITE REMEMBER YOUR LINE. CARD 4 IS THE STUDIO, THE OUTSIDE INFLUENCE THAT WILL TRY TO DICTATE HOW YOU LIVE YOUR LIFE. CARD 5 IS YOUR CLAIM TO FAME — WHAT WILL YOU BECOME KNOWN FOR?

56

SPIRIT SCALE

WHAT IS LIFE BUT A SONG? THIS SPREAD TAKES YOU THROUGH THE CLASSIC MUSICAL SCALE. EACH OF THESE NOTES ALSO CORRESPONDS WITH A CHAKRA POINT; THAT MEANS THAT EACH NOTE ALSO HAS A SPIRITUAL MEANING ATTACHED TO IT.

AS YOU DO THIS SPREAD, IT MAY HELP TO TREAT IT AS A KIND OF MEDITATION. GET INTO A COMFORTABLE POSITION, GROUND YOURSELF AND AS YOU LAY DOWN EACH CARD, IMAGINE A BRIGHT LIGHT FLOATING OVER EACH CHAKRA POINT. TO REALLY GET YOURSELF IN TUNE, TRY HUMMING EACH NOTE AS YOU LAY DOWN THE CARD!

1: C = THE HEART CHAKRA. THIS CARD TALKS ABOUT WHAT'S MOST DEAR TO YOUR HEART.

2: D = THE THROAT CHAKRA. THIS CARD TELLS YOU WHAT MESSAGE YOU CAN BRING TO THE WORLD.

3: E = THIRD EYE CHAKRA. THIS CARD UNVEILS WHAT YOUR INTUITION HAS BEEN TRYING TO TELL YOU.

4: F = THE CROWN CHAKRA. THIS CARD REVEALS WHAT YOU NEED TO MOVE BEYOND YOUR LIMITATIONS.

5: G = THE ROOT CHAKRA. THIS CARD IS WHAT YOU MUST HOLD ON TO TO STAY GROUNDED.

6: A = THE SACRAL CHAKRA. THIS CARD UNLOCKS THE SECRET OF CREATIVITY.

7: B = SOLAR PLEXUS CHAKRA. THIS CARD SHOWS WHAT YOU DRAW POWER FROM.

57

Page Right: *Mystical Medleys: A Vintage Cartoon Tarot*, Hall, G.

Of course, we all have different skillsets — even if you want to produce an oracle deck for publication, you may not feel like writing an accompanying guide falls within your remit. Some publishers will assign a staff member or freelance writer to the job; they may even (should your deck be a traditional tarot) have a generic book of definitions that can be published along with your deck. If you are publishing independently, then you might want to enlist the talent of a writer — but it will be helpful if they already have a good understanding of your cards and how you intend for them to be used.

During the creation of *The Fountain Tarot*, Jason Gruhl (writer) and Jonathan Saiz (artist) were both instrumental in the process of bringing life to the deck. It was not a case of Saiz painting the 78 images and Gruhl adding text after — and neither was it the other way around, with Gruhl dictating what he wanted in the cards due to having the greater experience of tarot. He and Jonathan were living in Mexico at the time, and they had a room set up for the painting of the project. Before they started designing, Jason created a matrix of all the decks he'd bought for research. Pasting them up in lines, he noted what was common in all of the cards, what was not repeated and what was random. He wanted to know which components, across time and decks, never shifted and shouldn't be messed with. He would then translate this to Jonathan, showing him what would need to be included and which elements could be reimagined.

Having worked less with tarot, Jonathan asked Jason to explain the mood of each card. He wanted to know what someone should feel when they picked each one up and the amount of emotion the card should evoke as a percentage: pure, overwhelming joy, as an example, would conjure up a different feeling to everyday contentment, which might be reserved for another card. Jason would provide him with the core symbols that must be included, his 'emotional percentage point', and then his own take on the card and how it might fit into the modern world. With this information, Jonathan would go to the studio and interpret this visually, through his own personal lens. Once he had returned with the painting, Jason would then get down to writing. The two of them would go back and forth, making tweaks to both the image and the words, so that the two artforms sat in harmony with one another.

It is important to remember that the person reading your guidebook may not have any knowledge of the subject you are writing about, and it's best not assume that they do. Monte Farber, who wrote the guidebook for *The Enchanted Tarot*, says: "It takes a thorough understanding of what you want to teach to be able to explain it simply, as if to a child. It requires clarity, brevity, and simplicity. It is imperative that a writer of an oracle system organize their book into clear, concise, and helpful guidance, so that readers don't just read it and put it down but refer to it for messages every day. You have got to keep the reader's point of view in mind at all times."

Page Left: Photography by May, L. Cards from *Mystical Medleys: A Vintage Cartoon Tarot*, Hall, G.

HOW TO STRUCTURE YOUR GUIDE

Books that accompany oracle and tarot decks these days vary greatly. A larger volume will go into a lot more depth than a small and compact guidebook, but, regardless of size, there are some sections that a reader will expect to see. The following list is a general summary for those unfamiliar with the structure of companion guides.

CONTENTS

The contents page is one of the most important parts of a guidebook because it will help a reader to locate the cards or different sections of the deck quickly. Your cards might be identified alphabetically or by number, and having them set out clearly and in order makes a big difference to how user-friendly your manual is. There is nothing worse for the reader than flipping back and forward through a book trying to find a specific card.

INTRODUCTION

An introduction is a good place to explain the ethos of the deck that the reader has in their hands. This could be an opportunity to speak about how the deck came to be or why it can be used as a powerful tool.

HISTORICAL OR RELEVANT SUBJECT INFORMATION

If a deck is based around the I-Ching, as an example, or is a traditional tarot or Lenormand, then you may wish to inform your reader of any significant historical context. This will not be relevant for all decks and is a matter of personal choice. Should you be creating a deck based on an artist's pre-existing artwork, a little information about their life might be desirable.

INSTRUCTIONS FOR USE

Not everyone who picks up your deck will have experience of divining and it is always useful to add tips about how they can use and care for it. Some authors might like to include examples of how a user can bond with their cards (such as connecting through ritual) and most will also include information about how to approach storing and cleansing them, how to shuffle, and any considerations that must be made before reading for someone else.

DEFINITIONS

The meanings associated with each card will make up the bulk of the book. How much text you allow for each card is dependent on how thick you wish your book to be. Whether you choose to include a paragraph for each card or a whole page, a title, meaning, reversed interpretation (if specific to your deck) and selection of keywords is usually enough to get a reader started. While not all books contain images, some will add a small greyscale illustration, making the card definitions identifiable and easy to refer to if the deck is not to hand. It can be frustrating for a reader to have to find the physical card when reading the book, so this is advantageous.

SPREADS

Spreads or methods for reading are an important inclusion, unless you are creating a deck of affirmation cards, for which this is not necessarily applicable. A spread will show a reader how to lay their deck and give them different options for doing so. Within the world of tarot, most books carry the traditional spreads, such as The Horseshoe and *The Celtic Cross*, but I have found that individual spreads, created by the author and specific to the deck, are usually more popular. For example, in the *Vintage Wisdom Oracle* by Victoria Moseley (U.S. Games, 2014), there are five spreads based around the style of the deck, *The Penny Farthing* Spread and *The Chatelaine Spread* being just two. Including specifically crafted spreads such as these will add to the style and individuality of your product. People will rightly feel as though they are getting more for their money and that care has been invested into the deck.

CONCLUSION

A conclusion is not essential, but it is a nice way of wrapping up your text. It can be as practical or flamboyant as you wish but will usually inspire the reader to start working with your cards and embark on an adventure with them.

AUTHOR BIO

Most books will have some kind of profile of the author or creator. This will likely include their background and information about previous works or notable achievements. If you have taught or presented relevant topics publicly, or have been interviewed on television or radio, then this kind of information should appear here. Your bio is often concluded with a sentence or two about where you are based. Any other social media handles and contact details can be placed at the end of this piece.

ARTIST BIO

As above, in the event that the artist and author are different.

INDEX

An index, which allows you to locate specific information within the book alphabetically, is desirable but not essential. If your guide is small, then this is probably unnecessary.

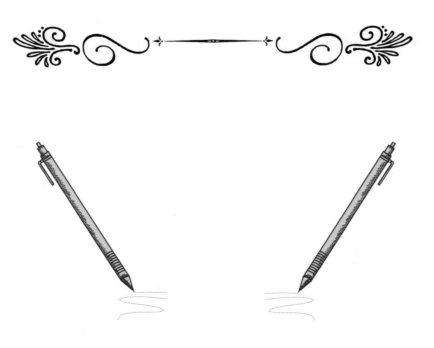

A DIGITAL BOOK

In order to cut costs, not all oracle and tarot manuals will be offered as a hard copy. These days, it is quite normal for accompanying literature to be sent as a PDF file or downloaded from the creator's website. Printing comes with cost and the bigger the volume, the greater the expense. This is worth considering if you intend to write a large companion guide. Some creators will offer the substantial 'little white book' but provide the option for an expanded text in a digital format. This can become part of the overall price or it might be sold as an optional extra for those who wish to deepen their knowledge about your deck.

There are pros and cons to doing this. While some will always prefer a physical book and find reading from a screen distracting or even uncomfortable, there will be those who like the convenience of being able to pull up the text on their phone or tablet while on the go, rather than carrying a manual about with them.

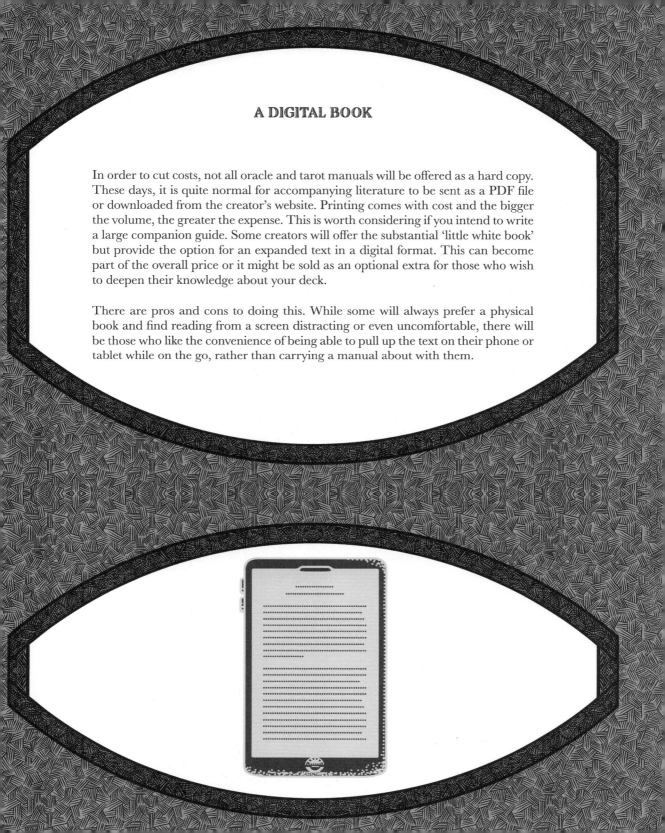

PUBLISHING YOUR ORACLE

Contents

Publishing is still one of the mysteries of the tarot and oracle world — and it's something that many new deck designers seek information about.

When most people think of publishing, it's the large companies that come to mind: U.S. Games Systems, Hay House, Llewellyn, Lo Scarabeo, and Schiffer are industry leaders. There are others, too, such as Blue Angel, Race Point, and Eddison Books, that are well-known for printing high quality tarot and oracle decks. Independent publishing houses, such as Liminal11, are also making big splashes within the industry, carefully choosing a smaller number of decks to publish in the space of a year but still making a large impact. The much-anticipated *Modern Witch Tarot*, created by Lisa Sterle and published by Liminal11, was one of the most successful decks of 2019, leading to it becoming nominated for, and winning, notable oracle awards alongside the offerings of larger, established publishers.

The advent of self-printing technology over the last 10 years has really opened the oracle deck world up to new creators. Many designers have bypassed traditional publishing houses and have decided to self-publish their work. There are advantages and disadvantages to all methods of publishing, depending on your motives for doing so, and we will look at these in this chapter.

Page Right:
Ethereal Visions: An Illuminated Tarot Deck, Hughes, M.
Tarot of Mystical Moments, Welz-Stein, C.
The Dreamkeepers Tarot, Huston, L.

TEN *of* PENTACLES

0 • THE FOOL

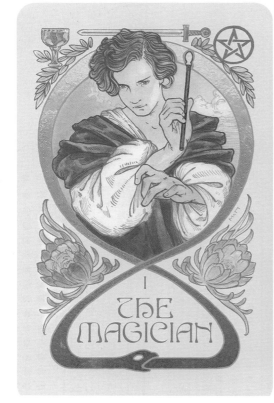

I
THE
MAGICIAN

QUEEN *of* CUPS

MASS-MARKET PUBLISHERS

HOW DO YOU CONTACT A LARGE PUBLISHING HOUSE?

Most large publishing houses will have their contact information listed on their website, along with a notice as to whether they are accepting submissions. It's probably best to email your proposals rather than sending hard copies through the post, although editors may respond with a request for a hard copy to be sent.

Most publishers will have guidelines in place for submissions, which must be adhered to and should be easy enough to locate on their website. It is important, firstly, to make sure that the publisher you contact prints the kind of deck you are proposing. Some mass-market publishers will save you time and effort by listing the kind of decks they are and are not interested in pursuing. Some focus on collectible tarot decks, others prefer original oracles. Once you've determined that the publisher you're interested in sells the kind of deck you have created, it will be up to you to explain your particular approach in your proposal.

A deck will not always need to be complete for a publisher to become interested, and it is not always necessary to show all the cards. If you're submitting a tarot, Llewellyn Books (as an example) asks that you provide two to three Major Arcana cards, a court card, and one pip from each suit. A cover letter and outline of the system is required, as you'd expect. Permissions for any work from other sources will need to be included and, if photographs of people are included in the work, releases will need to be obtained.

The outline of your system can be as detailed as you wish, though it is wise to be both brief and comprehensive. A publisher will want to know how the deck will work and why it will be of interest to their customers. Pitching is important, so be sure to outline your deck's goal and selling points. You've got a great product to sell, so sell them on it!

The example shown here, for *The Da Vinci Enigma Tarot* by Caitlin Matthews, is thorough and covers all of the information that a prospective publisher requires, listing the deck's background, structure, its uses, selling points, and an outline of the accompanying book. It also includes a short bio of the author.

Lynn Araujo
Director of Communications at U.S. Games

·◦~ᗴᘓᕤᕤᘓᗥ~◦·

The process of publishing is a mystery to many people. How might an artist become published by U.S. Games?

There are a number of different ways that deck projects get contracted for publication at U.S. Games. In the last few years, we have been more proactive in finding new artists and acquiring projects but, ten years ago, people would mostly send us proposals to be reviewed by our New Products Review Committee for consideration. Sometimes people send sample art; sometimes they have the entire deck finished. Generally, the more we see of a deck, the better. The committee is made up of people from the Art Department: our Creative Director and designers, our Acquisitions Manager, the Editor (myself), the Chairman, and people from the sales and marketing teams. We accept art submissions, but it needs to be presented as a concept with six sample cards.

Since there are so many artists working on [divinatory] art, it's a different scenario these days. There are several different paths for us to pursue new artists and new decks. In a few cases we have seen decks being launched independently (for example, on *Kickstarter* or *Indiegogo*). Sometimes, we will support these projects, chat with the creator, and — if we find common ground and think their deck would be a good fit for U.S. Games customers — we will offer a contract. They receive royalties with an advance. Some examples acquired this way have been *Crow Tarot, Field Tarot, Dreamkeepers Tarot*, and *Ethereal Visions Tarot*.

Other times we find artists on social media such as Instagram or Facebook, and initiate a dialogue about working on a project. We've also found artists through collaborative decks that have already been published. It's great when artists are already involved in tarot but, occasionally, we commission an artist who is just learning about it and so we try to provide more guidance. On some occasions, we publish an oracle deck by an artist to begin with, and then work with them to create a tarot deck. An example that comes to mind is Catrin Welz-Stein, a very talented collage artist. We published her oracle deck, *Oracle of Mystical Moments*, with some of her existing work. We then commissioned a tarot deck in the same evocative style.

Some artists, who have previously published their own deck, prefer to keep the design much the same — and we respect that choice — while many others put their complete faith in U.S. Games' experienced designers and editors, as they know we want to make the deck the best it can be. I know of several artists who were positively thrilled at the design changes we suggested. It is always a collaborative process. The deck creator always has the right to final approval.

THREE *of* PENTACLES

QUEEN *of* WANDS

What does U.S. Games look for in a new deck?

We are mostly interested in the quality of the artwork. We appreciate fine art that is well executed whether it is in paint, watercolor, ink, or digital. [In tarot decks, across both the Major and Minor cards, we look for excellent composition and consistency.] New concepts and themes should be supported by outstanding art and writing.

Is there a set process that all deck submissions go through at U.S. Games?

To a large extent, the timeframe between contract and submission of work is up to the artist. If they need 12 months, that's fine. If they need two to three years (if they're starting from scratch), we give them as much time as they need. Once we have the art and accompanying documents, we review them and let the artist know that everything has been accepted. There is usually a queue of projects in production, so it may be 3-12 months before production works begins. However, since we have hired more designers, we are shortening the time projects wait for production. The editing and design work for cards, guidebook, and box may take two to three months, and the artist and author will see everything before it goes to the printer. We usually get printer proofs one or two months later; these allow us to check that everything, such as [color], is as it should be. Sometime after that we will receive production samples. A few months later, the printed decks come in, which is always very exciting and gratifying.

Copyright is a hot topic within this industry. It has been common for independents to take a historic deck, such as the Rider-Waite-Smith Tarot, and reprint it, often with an added filter. As an organization, what guidelines do you have around the illegal printing of your decks?

U.S. Games Systems holds the copyright to the Rider-Waite-Smith deck until 2022. We do legally pursue those entities that are producing counterfeits. We are particularly aggressive (having our lawyers sending cease and desist letters) when our artists' work is being stolen and counterfeited. It's so terribly unfair to them and completely unethical. Our artists are part of our family, so we feel strongly about protecting their work.

What advice would you give to anyone who is interested in creating a tarot or oracle deck?

Creating a tarot or oracle deck is a massive undertaking, so make sure it's something you are ready to put your heart and soul into. I've been working on my own tarot deck with the artist Lisa Hunt for over five years, and it's been a real pleasure. It is important that you create what you feel passionate about, but try to make it relatable as well. Readers … like to see and read about your original interpretations, but they have to be able to relate to the imagery for themselves. For an oracle deck, of course, there are fewer restrictions than with tarot or Lenormand. We like our decks to have at least 40 cards and have some cohesive unifying theme and narrative.

WILL A PUBLISHER HANDLE PUBLICITY AND MARKETING?

This is not true of all publishing houses, and publishers will usually have some requirements of the creator or artist. While some do have a large publicity machine behind them, a creator cannot rely on the publisher alone to get the word out there. As the deck creator, you understand the work best — so you also understand who will want to use your deck because you're among your target audience!

Some publishers will request that you fill in a marketing questionnaire, and your answers will be used for publicity and promotional tools. This will include your own ideas about the selling and marketing of your deck — in order for the publisher to understand the target customer — and the top selling points of your work. You may have your own ideas about the buying market and where it might be best to promote; a deck based around manga, as an example, might be as successful at comic conventions as it will be at an esoteric or spiritual fair. For those in a different global location to the publisher, local and relevant information is invaluable because it can help a marketing team to target specific events that could be helpful in the sale of your title.

Your own social media profile could be helpful in publicizing your deck and in reaching those who might find it interesting. If they are savvy, most publishers will want to take advantage of this. Some will require you to list shops that are willing to stock your deck, contact popular reviewers, and cite publications that would be interested in using your cards in their features.

Regardless of the publisher, it is never advisable to sit back and hope that they will do all of the work. Since the release of my own deck and tarot book (*Tarot: Your Personal Guide,* 2018), I have controlled much of my own publicity, from book and deck signings at events to articles in some of the most well-distributed New Age magazines. I have also spoken about the *Spirit Within Tarot* on radio shows; recently, on one with 247,000 listeners at the time. This can be a great opportunity for you to explain the unique selling points of your cards.

WILL HAVING YOUR DECK PUBLISHED BY A BIG PUBLISHING HOUSE MAKE YOU RICH?

There will always be creators who do well from having their deck published, but this is dependent on distribution and, in some cases, the popularity of the person creating it. Some decks are more commonplace and are available in high-street-chain booksellers. Established artists, such as Ciro Marchetti, do well because of their popularity but also because they supplement their revenue stream with related merchandise and services. This is true of many creators whose decks have highlighted other marketable assets for the publisher to commission and develop — journals, books, and spin-off decks can be produced off the popularity of just one deck.

Lynn Araujo, Editorial and Communications Director at U.S. Games Systems, says: "We must not underestimate how financially successful even a new tarot artist can become. When U.S. Games started becoming more proactive in their acquisitions a few years ago, we discovered some amazing talent by artists who hadn't even considered creating tarot decks, and now they are very successful. One example is Catrin Welz-Stein, whose *Oracle of Mystical Moments* became such a big hit that folks clamored for her subsequent tarot deck. Because of our strong network of international distributors and publishers, we not only sell decks to a worldwide market but also sell foreign rights to publishers around the world, and this is very lucrative for creators. Several of our popular decks are also being published in Russia, France, Italy, Asia [and] Israel, to name but a few. The creators receive a significant profit from these foreign rights contracts."

The success of a deck, financially or otherwise, can vary depending on the publishing house. U.S. Games Systems is an established company and has been selling specialty playing cards for over 40 years, while Hay House has a vast and generous distribution, meaning that their decks can be found in a wide range of bookstores for affordable prices. This means that a greater volume can be sold, and larger profits generated, for the creator. Not all deals may be as lucrative as these: some creators will receive smaller financial returns from their publisher, even if their deck proves to be successful.

Amy Zerner

Creator of *The Enchanted Love Tarot*

Page Right: *The Wild Goddess Oracle*, Zerner, A. and Farber, M.

Which deck did you release first, and how did it come to be published?

In 1988, Penguin Books published my partner Monte Farber's first book and card deck about astrology, *Karma Cards: A Guide to Your Future Through Astrology*, which was translated into eighteen languages and is still in print. In 1989, Monte and I had our first opportunity to work together. I leapt at the chance when Eddison/Sadd Editions — who helped Monte bring *Karma Cards* into the world — gave us the opportunity to create The Enchanted Tarot book and tarot deck set, with Monte writing the book text and me creating 78 of my fabric collage tapestries that were then photographed and reproduced in miniature (first published by St. Martin's Press and now Quarto).

By the time we were working on *The Enchanted Tarot*, we were already confident enough about the way it could and should be done; so, for our next project, *The Alchemist: The Formula for Turning Your Life to Gold*, we decided to become book packagers ourselves. We did not really [know] how we were going to do it but went ahead and got the deal anyway. Thankfully, the legendary editor Thomas Dunne, of St. Martin's Press, saw in us the spark of something. This gave him the confidence to let us do it on our own, for which we will be eternally grateful.

Together, just the two of us, we have invented, written, illustrated, designed, and arranged for the manufacture and delivery of many of our oracle titles to various publishers around the world. Some publishers that we have worked with include Simon & Schuster for our *Psychic Circle*, Weiser books for *Instant Tarot*, Sterling Publishing for *Little Reminders: Law of Attraction Oracle Cards*, *The Enchanted Spellboard*, and *The Truth Fairy Pendulum Kit*, and Schiffer Publishing for *Enchanted Love Tarot* and *The Creativity Oracle*.

We divide the required tasks according to our abilities and interests but make all decisions together. In addition to our more traditionally creative roles, I have applied my artistic skills to all of our time scheduling and production while Monte acts as our agent, lawyer, and typist.

How has deck publishing changed since you released your first deck?

There were only a handful of new tarot and oracle titles being published back when we started: *The Medicine Cards* and *The Mythic Tarot* come to mind. There are also quite a few that defy categorization. Using Google, all you have to do is type in "tarot deck" and

then stand back — a virtual torrent of tarot decks will appear. Publishing has changed dramatically over the years. We used to have our titles picked up by book clubs; that would add another 50,000 copies to our first printings. Those days are gone. Publishers are very careful nowadays and publish far fewer books than they used to.

Can you describe the mainstream publishing process from the perspective of the creator?

Firstly, a proposal would be submitted to an editor. It takes time to go through the acquisitions process where the team at the publishing house (sales and editorial) meet periodically to discuss new projects and ideas that the editor might like. They're super busy and need to know certain things before they can agree to commit their time to reading a pitch. Once that is done, you will have to write a cover letter to explain yourself and your proposal. This submission is usually done through a literary agent but, in our case, we [represent] ourselves.

Sometimes the editor or publisher will request additional content or a tweaking of the proposal. If you are lucky enough to get an acceptance of your submission, then it takes time to get a contract. The publishing business has seasons and lists, so for instance, to publish in January, they would need a final manuscript and files in late spring.

Our relationship with the many publishers and editors we have worked with over the years is very special. There is a mutual respect for the creativity that our various jobs entail. We always try to be on time with delivery dates and work hard to support our titles and the publishers expect that. We think of our projects as our babies and they require a lot of care and nurturing!

What are the benefits of becoming published by a mainstream publisher?

Distribution. Distribution. Distribution!

Have you experienced any difficulties with mainstream publishing?

Rejection is hard. To live creatively requires as much bravery as it does dedication and wonderful ideas. But you can't really take it personally: sometimes, it is just a matter of timing or trends. We don't give up if we really believe in a project. Sometimes it gets rejected but then we sell it years later. We have even sold projects to a publisher who had initially rejected them!

What advice would you give to anyone seeking deck publishing from a publishing company?

I cannot stress enough the importance of professionalism. Have someone review and copyedit your pages and give you feedback. And please keep in mind that no matter how great and interesting you think your story is, the first question any publisher is going to ask is: "Who wants to buy this book and why do they want to buy it?" This is another way of saying: "Why should I risk a bunch of my limited capital publishing this and not something else?" It is your job to convince them. Also, your bio is important. Publishers like authors with a platform, meaning a cool website, social networking and status in their industry.

What advice, as a creative, would you give to someone creating an oracle or tarot deck?

Be original.

The Magician
1

ENERGY

The Chariot
7

DETERMINATION

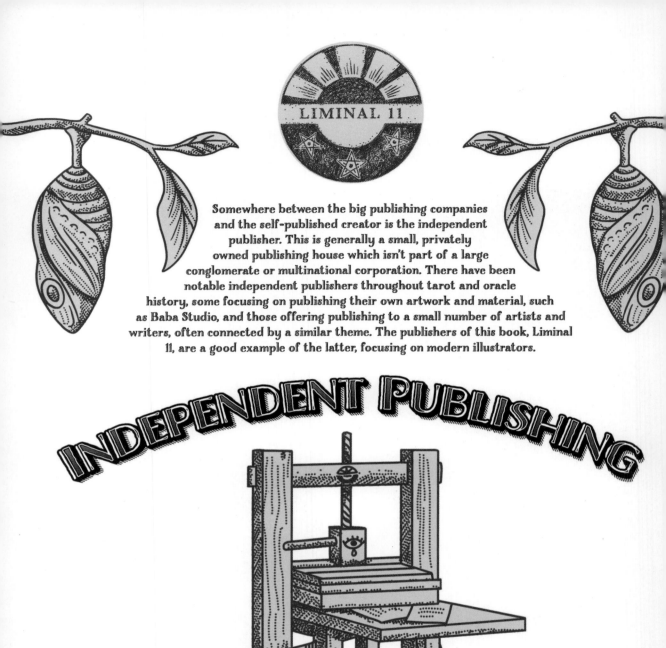

Somewhere between the big publishing companies and the self-published creator is the independent publisher. This is generally a small, privately owned publishing house which isn't part of a large conglomerate or multinational corporation. There have been notable independent publishers throughout tarot and oracle history, some focusing on publishing their own artwork and material, such as Baba Studio, and those offering publishing to a small number of artists and writers, often connected by a similar theme. The publishers of this book, Liminal 11, are a good example of the latter, focusing on modern illustrators.

INDEPENDENT PUBLISHING

Darren Shill, one of the founding members of Liminal 11, describes the difference between independent and mass-market publishers as such: "An independent publisher needs a strong identity to find a voice alongside the larger companies. It achieves this by having a clear genre that it works in and a very specific production value that it applies. That way, people know what to expect when picking up a publication from that indie publisher and will hopefully look out for their future work."

Because they are independent, these publishers produce fewer products than mass-market publishing, as Darren explains: "That means they take greater risk by having fewer titles from which to generate a bestseller, but it also means that they can really focus on all the works they are supporting." And yet, the smaller size of independent publishing houses can be a real boon. "One advantage that indie publishers have, which all small businesses benefit from, is speed of decision making. With just one or two people making a decision on commissioning a work, the time taken to get a work agreed on and started is massively reduced. Instinct drives decisions rather than group thought."

Co-founders Darren Shill and Kay Medaglia met many years ago at a comics discussion group based in the London comic store Gosh! Kay was running the group with a friend of Darren's, and, due to their strong passion for comics, the two stayed in touch afterwards. On checking Kay's website one day to see what was new, Darren noticed someone had suggested that Kay create a tarot deck. "I have been a tarot reader for about 30 years and had built quite the collection of crowdfunded decks by this point, so this immediately struck me as just about the best idea possible," reminisces Darren. "Kay's work is amazingly warm, inclusive, and deeply grounded by Zen Buddhism. This seemed the perfect opportunity to create a deck with compassion at its core — one that was welcoming and that might open the tarot up to a new audience. This was to be *The Luna Sol Tarot*."

"I approached Kay with various ways of creating the deck, such as crowdfunding; but the most ambitious, and the one that stuck, was starting a whole new publisher. We had too many other amazing projects we wanted to do, plus there was the sense that what we learnt from the first tarot deck could be used on the next one and so on – perfecting production, design and the guidebook layout as we did so."

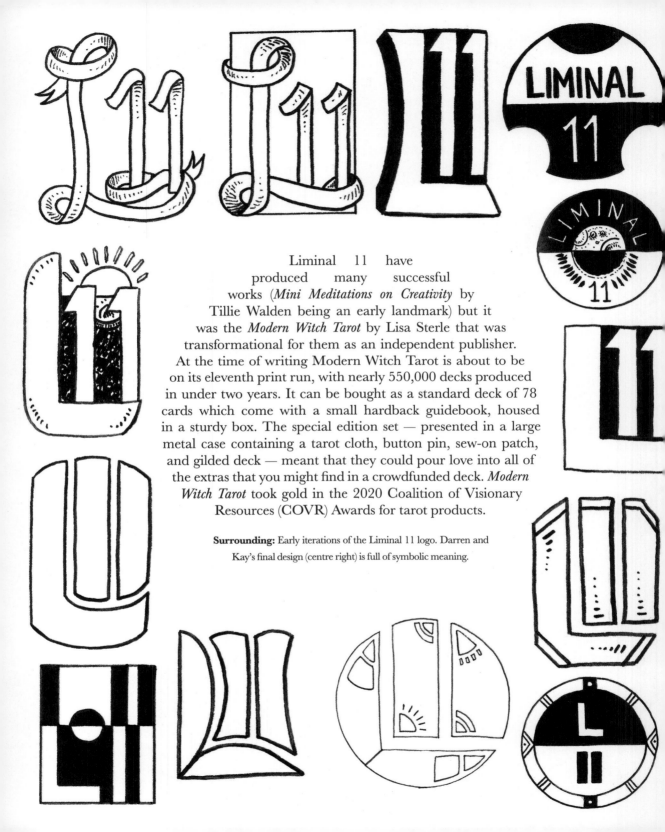

Liminal 11 have produced many successful works (*Mini Meditations on Creativity* by Tillie Walden being an early landmark) but it was the *Modern Witch Tarot* by Lisa Sterle that was transformational for them as an independent publisher. At the time of writing Modern Witch Tarot is about to be on its eleventh print run, with nearly 550,000 decks produced in under two years. It can be bought as a standard deck of 78 cards which come with a small hardback guidebook, housed in a sturdy box. The special edition set — presented in a large metal case containing a tarot cloth, button pin, sew-on patch, and gilded deck — meant that they could pour love into all of the extras that you might find in a crowdfunded deck. *Modern Witch Tarot* took gold in the 2020 Coalition of Visionary Resources (COVR) Awards for tarot products.

Surrounding: Early iterations of the Liminal 11 logo. Darren and Kay's final design (centre right) is full of symbolic meaning.

Darren Shill
Co-founder of Liminal 11

What inspired you to set up an independent publishing company?

Self-publishing through crowdfunding sites is great, but we also wanted our works to be easily available through shops, especially those dear to our heart like the London shops Gosh!, Watkin's Books, and Atlantis. We also wanted a long life to our titles. Where do you sell once the crowdfunding campaign is over? How do you attract people to your webshop when it's not part of a larger platform? That longevity is important. We can build a sense of what to expect from a Liminal 11 publication and can feed the success from one work back into supporting more amazing creators, too. It's hopefully something of a virtuous circle!

How would you describe Liminal 11?

Liminal 11 is an indie Mind, Body & Spirit publisher creating products of benefit to the world. We have a strong focus on illustration, especially from comics artists, and tarot is at our core.

What obstacles have you come up against as an independent publisher?

One of the biggest hurdles is distribution. A distributor will want to look at your lineup of titles and possibly see how well they are doing before taking you on. Which, of course, makes sense as there are only so many companies they can represent. This means, however, that we had to commission and self-distribute a range of publications before reaching that point — a big financial risk for Liminal 11 and a huge act of faith from our creators.

Having the UK distributor Turnaround take us on was a big moment. We had introduced ourselves at a very early stage when our products were wonderful concepts rather than a reality. But we got along straight away — they were supporting some of the indie publishers we loved, such as Avery Hill, and they clearly had a serious passion for their publishers.

The comics convention Thought Bubble 2018 was a launching point for our first lineup, including *The Luna Sol Tarot*. I was doing free tarot readings for anyone who bought the deck, which I always do at conventions, and did a reading for someone at Turnaround. That reading was unusual and somewhat uncanny! The following week, having seen Liminal's beautiful works doing so well in the wild, Turnaround offered us distribution.

The other hurdle as a new publisher is getting your name out there. By which I mean, getting known by retailers, suppliers and, most importantly, tarot readers. Having a very

specific type of deck we wanted to create helped there. But the other early boost we had was working with Sarah Wray, our marketing manager. Sarah has worked in publishing for some time and has excellent connections. She is also one of the most professional people I know! Liminal wouldn't be where it is without her.

What has been rewarding about independent publishing?

One of the most wonderful things is seeing the response to our decks. The Luna Sol sold out in the first six months and was incredibly well received by both the notable figures in the tarot community — such as Benebell Wen, Jessica Dore and Michelle Tea — and also with tarot readers who gave us such lovely feedback. Hearing a professional reader say that it was now their deck of choice with clients, as it was so approachable and compassionate, meant the world to us.

Then the scale of the response from *Modern Witch Tarot* took our breath away! Both this and *The Luna Sol Tarot* had strong diversity and inclusivity — that this was championed and so warmly appreciated by fans and reviewers was everything to us.

How does a creator come to design for Liminal 11?

Like any indie publisher we are very choosy in the decks we back. If we can only publish a very small number a year, every deck we publish is potentially at the expense of another; so we spend a lot of thought on who is a good fit for Liminal 11, and whether we are the best publisher for them.

It's a blend of both us seeking out creators and people approaching us, although predominantly we commission the work. When looking for decks to commission we keep a close eye on social media to see if anything exciting is emerging. We spotted *Modern Witch Tarot* when Lisa had shared just three cards on Instagram. We also keep a keen eye out at the tarot and comics conventions we attend.

If someone approaches us, then a good representative sample of the deck is very useful — so, a few Major Arcana and at least one pip and court card. They certainly don't need a full deck. A written description of the essence of the deck and inspiration behind the work is helpful too.

What do you look for in new deck creators?

First off, we need to have a connection. That's tricky to describe, but I think a tarot reader will know what we mean: a gut feeling, a tingling of intuition. Strong art is obviously essential — this is a visual medium — but it is more than that. Does it hold the eye and trigger something? Is it cohesive? Could you actually read with this deck? The other important thing we consider is whether the creator's voice takes the conversation further; by which we mean, are they adding something new to the tarot world?

Is there a set fee for deck creators?

We pay an advance, which can vary a bit depending on the scope of the work, plus royalties on the net receipts from the work. The advance can be useful cashflow for the creator when they are working on the deck.

What advice would you give to someone wanting to design a tarot or oracle deck?

Try to approach the cards as one continuous project. Dedicate around six months, if you can, to completing the deck. That way they will feel cohesive and like they come from one place in time. I remember talking to the wonderful Geraldine of Atlantis at the 2018 London Tarot Conference after she had just used The *Luna Sol Tarot* in a workshop. She asked: "How long did it take to create *The Luna Sol*?" "Five months of dedicated time," I answered. "It shows, they work!" she replied.

These days, the number of self-published decks available outweighs the new releases offered from publishing companies. While there are a greater number of publishers releasing tarot and oracle decks than there were 20 years ago, the amount of people releasing their own creations has skyrocketed. In some cases, these independent decks have gained more success than their mass-market cousins.

Self-publishing is not for the fainthearted. In fact, it can take a great reserve of strength and a thick skin to deal with the many occupational hats you'll be required to wear. As well as being the creator, you'll also be the administrator, the publicist, the packer — and not to mention, in control of the finances. It might be you who receives the glory when everything goes well, but it is also you that people come to when there is a fault or complaint. Of course, this is not intended to discourage the eager self-publisher but is simply a heads-up. Self-publishing, even when done well, is an exhausting process and will take up a lot of time and energy — physically, mentally, and emotionally.

As with all methods of publishing, research is paramount. Thankfully, because so many people have trod this ground before, there are plenty of testimonials and blog posts out there by self-publishers. It can help you to do a bit of research and follow creators that have found success in self-publishing. They will often share tips on their platforms and will occasionally host Q&As where their followers can ask questions about the process. Many printers are contactable through social media, too, and will have examples and testimonials to share from satisfied artists.

Self-publishing will allow complete control of a project. A publisher may want to alter certain details or may not wish to financially commit to specific designs. Taking the self-publishing route offers free creative license; however, this does come at a cost. Unless you have a lump sum to invest in your deck or are willing to seek out a loan, it might mean seeking other methods of financing the project.

Jason Gruhl
Creator of *The Fountain Tarot*

How did The Fountain Tarot come to be?

Jonathan is a fine artist by trade, and he was looking for a new project to work on. We happened to be on vacation in Mexico at the time. I'd brought my tarot deck along with me — The *Robin Wood Tarot* — and I suggested we do a reading about what his next project should be. I laid out the cards on the bed in the hotel room, and he literally put his hand on my chest and said: "Oh my God, I want to make a tarot deck and you can write the book, and we can ask Andi to design the box." I thought that the idea sounded amazing. He had wanted to do something different from the usual large canvases he'd been creating, and this allowed for him to totally immerse himself in this world.

I had used tarot since college, but I didn't really know what I had in that deck; I would bring it out with friends and I'd take it to parties for entertainment, but it wasn't until we started working on *The Fountain Tarot* that I began to dive into hundreds of years of tarot history to find out what it truly is. For my research, I bought many decks — classic and contemporary — which helped me to consider why certain aspects landed for me personally, and why other approaches did not. It was really important that the cards had an intimate experience with the user, so that reading them would feel more like a conversation rather than being told to do something. I spent time looking at how well other decks did that. You could appreciate some of them for their beauty, others for their esotericism and how deep they'd go into the symbols included on each of the cards. In doing this, we were able to think about what we really wanted to accomplish.

I often think that knowing what you do not want is as important as knowing what you do, because there are so many choices to make at the beginning. Figuring out *what this deck wasn't* was a really important part of the process. We decided that we would not focus on numerology or esoteric symbols. Instead, we intended for it to be more of a visceral experience for the reader. We also wanted to keep it modern, rather than using people or objects that do not exist in this age. We kept the traditional names as a reference point, but we decided to feature people we could all [recognize] such as friends, aunts, and people down the block.

Why did you choose to self-publish?

We didn't understand anything about the publishing world at that point. However, one of the main reasons for self-publishing was because we wanted to control as many elements as possible. Due to how detail-oriented Andi is, she researched what we needed to do and got to it. It was Andi who found an American company that contracts with Chinese factories. They acted as a broker and found us a factory that would be able to offer all of the different features we required.

I am a pretty sustainable guy and like to shop close to home, so I was not keen on printing so far away to begin with. However, the deck would have cost $70 to buy if we had printed it here in the States. We wanted *The Fountain Tarot* to be accessible to everyone, so printing in China lowered the final retail price to $40. The broker found a factory that could agree to many of the design features we wanted — such as the silver gilding, the box with the magnetic clasp, and foiling — and produce them all in the one place. In the United States, we would have had to work with a handful of different factories to accommodate all of them. We made our own checks and found out that the factory chosen had ethical certification, which was very important to us, too.

How long did the process take?

It was definitely about a year and a few months of painting for Jonathan. It required about three or four months of solid research, and eight or nine months of writing. Altogether, it must have taken about a year and a half to create everything. To Kickstart it and get it out to people probably took about nine months to a year. So, the whole process — from sitting on the bed and thinking about it to production — was about two and a half years.

How does self-publishing work?

The big concern, when self-publishing, is how you are going to pay for it. To begin with, we had to figure out all of the elements we wanted to be in this deck. We had a conversation with the intermediary company (who were responsible for working with the different printer companies) so that they could find a printer that would be able to produce a quality product. So, I'd advise spending time looking at all of the different features, such as card stock. Once you have found the right printer, you must then discuss the different price points with them. For example, if you want 5,000 decks with all of your desired features, you will need to know what it is going to cost you.

Financially, there is much to consider, including the printing, design, the setup for the initial prototypes, the shipping costs, and the tariffs and taxes. Because we used a broker, we needed to add their fee to the lot as well. Like many, we didn't have $25,000 to invest in the project, so we took the Kickstarter route to fund the entire production. We eventually made $28,000, which covered all of our expenses — for making this deck and distributing it — leaving a couple of thousand dollars for taxes, etc.

Once all of the paintings were complete, Jonathan and Andi photographed them in the Mexican sun and turned them into digital files. Andi then set to work on the box design, making it up in cardboard and figuring out the specs, which was then sent off in order for the factory to construct the prototype. When it first came back, there were things that didn't work — parts were [off-center], some of the edges had a little nick on the side, and

THE HIGH PRIESTESS II

THE TOWER XVI

THE MOON XVIII

THE LOVERS VI

QUEEN OF COINS

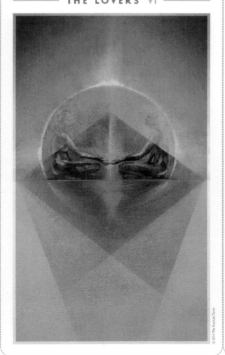

SIX OF SWORDS

the gilding came off on our hands — so we needed to stand strong and say that it was not good enough. When we got the second prototype back, it was pristine. We were then able to say to go ahead. It probably took about four months to receive the first print run. If it is over January, which is Chinese New Year, everything shuts down, so it is good to consider timing. This quick turnaround is one advantage to self-publishing.

Once we had all of our decks, the majority of sales went through our website, though we reached out to stores as well. We had 5,000 decks printed for our $25,000 investment and about 361 people backed the Kickstarter. When customers started purchasing the remaining decks, we were then able to start putting money aside. Because we printed in China, the decks cost $3.80 apiece to make and they were then sold at a $40 price-point. We were able to save some of our returns from that for the next print run of 5,000.

We packaged everything. We were able to set up an appointment with the U.S. postal service and they walked us through what we needed to do. We were able to print labels from home. If you have over 100 packages, we found out that they will send you a car to avoid taking up time at the post office.

None of us were going to retire off the back of this deck but we were able to make some money from doing it. We each probably received about $30,000 per year after the Kickstarter but, because it was our full-time job for that period, it's questionable as to whether the income matched the amount of work and effort that went into it. In the end, we sold 10,000 copies before the title was picked up by Shambhala Publications. After a number of years, we felt that we had done all we could with the deck and that our reach was limited. Because we wanted The Fountain Tarot to last and to continue permeating the world, this was the next logical step. Penguin Random House is the distributor, so it has now been able to reach every country in the world. It is one of Shambhala's top sellers.

What difficulties or obstacles did you face through self-publishing?

Because there were three of us, it made many aspects of the process pretty painless for me. Andi was very good at finding the right people and then bringing them to task. Working as a group, each with our own strengths, made a big difference. Finding out what your limitations are at the beginning can be helpful, especially if you want to build up contacts around you to help in those areas. Anytime that there was communication needed, Andi and Jonathan would push me forward as they saw me as the friendly face who knew what to say. However, when there was detail-oriented stuff that needed sorting and I might be too accommodating or nice, Andi would push me aside and say: "This is my deal." We had an obligation to the people who would eventually own the deck, and so we were fighting for them to have the best experience they could.

Page Left: *The Fountain Tarot*, Gruhl J., Saiz J., and Todaro A.

Is there a lot of administration when self-publishing?

In self-publishing there is a lot of administration because you are dealing with it all yourself. We tried to be as generous as we could be with regard to complaints. We'd always mail off a card if one needed to be replaced and we set aside spare decks for that. Over years of doing this, it did start to eat into our finances, so we'd still send them happily but asked if people would pay us a buck for the postage. I'm not built for mistrust, so I would always try my best to satisfy those who said they'd received a damaged or faulty deck.

What was the most rewarding part of self-publishing?

Just taking something from an idea to completion and being able to hold it and know you had a hand in its construction. It is amazing to be able to create something that other people find valuable and which hopefully impacts their life. Self-publishing made a lot of difference to this because every piece of that deck was what we wanted, and we didn't have to compromise anything for a publisher.

What advice would you give to anyone who wishes to self-publish?

Ask yourself if the world really needs it. Sometimes, not every idea needs to be made and not every proposal is a good one. It can help if you find a way of putting one sample deck together: then you can see if it is just for you, for your friends, for a community, or for the world. If you go through all of this and feel that it still needs to be distributed widely, then you can start finding those people who can help you fulfil your dream. Intention is important. Our energy becomes embedded in the things we create. You need to be straight with yourself and the reasons why you want to do it.

CROWD-FUNDING

Crowdfunding is a way of raising a large amount of money from a group of investors. Each person contributes a small amount of the overall cost to the production of the project, allowing for something, such as a deck, to become funded prior to printing. For those who cannot afford to self-publish alone, this is a good way of financing a project, but it can also help a creator to see how much interest a finished product would garner. Crowdfunding has become a popular way of raising money, but not only for decks. It allows people to promote and gain funding for many other forms of creative projects such as comics, art, theatre, and music. However, there are a number of things that one must consider before embarking on the creation of a campaign.

The most well-known crowdfunding platforms for deck creating are Kickstarter and Indiegogo. The sites are not webstores but act as a platform for a creator to reach backers who wish to pledge money in receipt of an eventual product of the project — in this case, a deck of cards. Many creators will add additional rewards to their campaign. For example, some investors will only pledge the price of one finished deck; but if you invest a greater sum, there are advantages to doing so. A creator might choose to lower the unit price of the deck if you buy more than one, add novelties such as spread cloths or a book, or even deliver in-person readings or include original artwork as an option for those who contribute the most. It gives a backer greater incentive to pledge a larger sum and feel part of the overall process. A lot of the extras will be limited or one-of-a-kind features, only available for the period that the crowdfunding campaign is live.

Kickstarter developed an all-or-nothing rule when they launched in 2009 which is intended to protect creators and backers, minimizing risks for both. The funds will not be released until the project has reached its goal, which means that creator or backer cannot lose out. If the goal is not reached, then the project does not go ahead. At the time of this writing, only 44% of projects reach their goal.

One of the most important things that a creator must consider ahead of starting a Kickstarter campaign is how much money they will actually need, because incorrect research can cost them heavily in the long run. If certain fees are not taken into account or are poorly estimated, this could result in a project not gaining as much of a financial investment as it requires. In this instance, you will still be obligated to fulfill your promise and cover the difference. When excited about birthing a new deck and sharing it with the world, not everyone is as meticulous as they need to be, so it is vital that you work out every single one of your costs beforehand. For example, the pricing of postage will vary depending where in the world you are sending your deck, and if this is not calculated accurately, it could easily eat into your profits. Campaigners who have not done their homework ahead of time have been burnt this way, causing them to make less profit and, in some cases, experience personal financial losses. We must remember that Kickstarter is a unique and valuable platform for the creator but, if not handled with caution, could result in debt. While it might not be recommended that a person asks for too much, it could make sense to ask for a little bit more than you think you'll need to cover any additional or unexpected costs.

Part of creating a successful campaign lies in building an audience prior to launch. As with any self-published deck creation, where marketing is essential without a publishing team behind you, it is important to lay the foundations before you announce your crowdfunding proposal. Social media is usually the best place to do something like this: starting up groups on Facebook for discussion or accounts on a platform like Instagram, for instance. The use of hashtags, and contacting big names within the industry, can make a big difference to the exposure of your project. This is a way of attracting potential backers before you even launch; a far better approach than starting your campaign without planning and just hoping that people will find it.

Starting a project on something like Kickstarter is relatively easy. To begin with, you must be over 18 years old. Upon opening an account, you will be asked to provide a photograph of your proposed project and a title, which becomes the URL for your campaign page. Most creators add some kind of promotional video of their deck. This can be a practical show-and-tell, describing the deck's unique selling points, or it might build interest through a short but intriguing teaser. Some creators will include eye-catching and luxurious 'mini movies', intended to encourage hype and excitement around their deck; these videos usually present just a few cards and use animation and mood to provoke their audience. It has been estimated that 20% more Kickstarter campaigns are successfully funded because of the inclusion of a video. As well as promotional media, the product description allows for you to explain more fully what you require backing for, and how you intend to use the backers' money.

An Amazon Payments business account is mandatory for processing credit transactions and receiving funds, and this can take up to seven days to be set up.

Page Right: Photography by May, L. Cards from *Golden Constellation Oracle Deck*, Gonzalez, A. and *White Numen: A Sacred Animal Tarot*, Gonzalez, A.

Amazon will take 3.5% of your funding for this service. All in all, because the Kickstarter team personally vet each project, it can take up to two working days to be approved. Once you get the green light, you can go live at any time. You will still be able to upload and make changes to your campaign, though the goal and end date cannot be altered. You will have the ability to update your information, and emails will be sent to all backers accordingly to notify them of any changes.

The funding duration can last up to 60 days, but Kickstarter recommends that you choose under 30 — a sense of urgency will encourage more people to back your deck. After the funding duration has ended, if you were lucky enough to achieve your goal, it will take two weeks for you to receive the money for your project. Kickstarter will collect a 5% fee, so be sure to factor this into your budget as well.

Indiegogo is less limiting than Kickstarter. There is no approval process for projects and no requirement regarding what you wish to fund. Indiegogo also accepts PayPal, and your funding campaign can be flexible, meaning that even if you do not reach your goal, you can still keep the money. This, of course, can be risky if your funding is not enough to cover your costs. While Indiegogo's commission is lower than Kickstarter's (just 4% of the overall funding), Indiegogo will raise this to 9% if your goal is not funded.

Page Left: Photography by Bright, S. Cards from *The New Chapter Tarot*. Briggs, K.

Dream up a project

Build an audience prior to launch

Carefully consider how much money you will need to make the project a reality

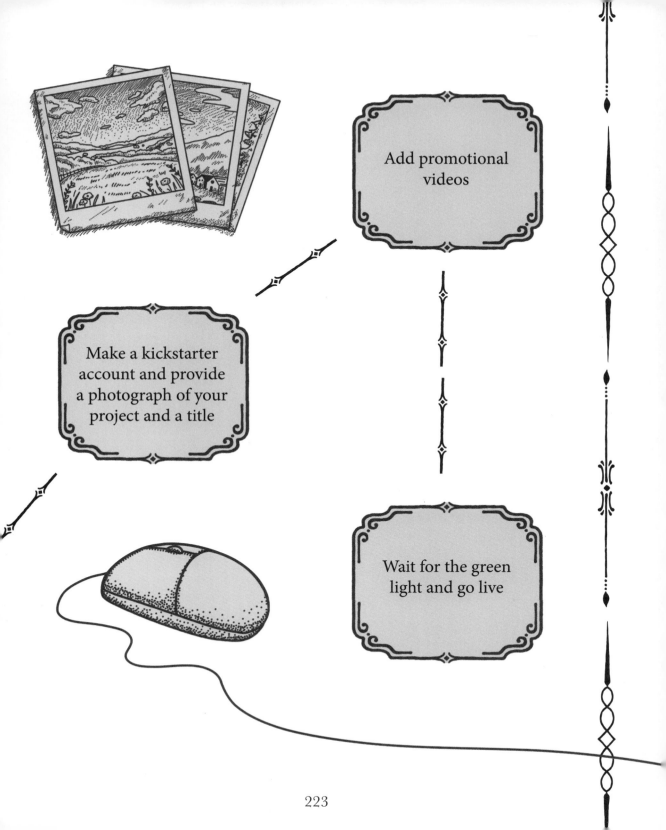

Add promotional videos

Make a kickstarter account and provide a photograph of your project and a title

Wait for the green light and go live

Andrea Aste and Neil Kelso
Creators of *Oracolarium*

Page Right: *Oracularium*, Aste, A. and Kelso, N.

Why did you decide to create a Kickstarter for your deck rather than choosing one of the other options available?

Working with a crowdfunding model is a good way to fund quite unusual projects. With platforms like Kickstarter, you can connect with people from around the world who have a niche interest, and who might be interested [in collaborating and participating] in the process of bringing something to life.

The other possible routes would be to completely self-finance the whole project (which gives fullest creative freedom but might be prohibitively expensive) or to work with a publisher (which offers the ability to work with an experienced team, but also might mean the project is constrained by the publisher's commercial prerogatives). We chose Kickstarter so we could talk directly to our customers throughout the process.

How does a Kickstarter work?

Before starting a Kickstarter project, it's important to have a very clear vision of your finished product. Kickstarter might not be the best route for everyone, so think carefully about whether it's the right model for you. Once you have your clear vision, the entire campaign must be created in advance and this is an enormous amount of work. You will need to design the whole product and know the exact cost of every component. In the case of a deck of cards, you must know the printing process in depth, so you are accurately calculating the costs of printing the cards, the box, the book, and the other materials. You will need to be certain that you are working in the correct resolution, file types, and [color] profiles. Even for an experienced professional graphic designer, this is a significant undertaking.

At this point, you should approach various printers and compare quotes so that you can be sure you are selecting the right paper stock and the right printing technology. This will also include considering how you will get the printed product to your customer, no matter where they are in the world. The logistics are a huge aspect of any Kickstarter campaign, and this is often the most expensive part of a project when customers are worldwide. There are some fees that Kickstarter retains. This is a small percentage of the money, but you must remember them in your calculations. Even currency exchange-rate fluctuations need to be kept in mind.

You will need to create your prototype product so that potential backers can see exactly

WANDERING

what they will receive. This must be absolutely faithful to the end product so your campaign is completely honest, and backers have a clear understanding of what you will be giving them for their money.

As well as your product, a Kickstarter campaign can offer other rewards to your backers — this rewards people who invest more. For example, for *Oracolarium*, we offered a variety of additional rewards including a reading cloth, a special wooden box, artwork, video tutorials and much more. If you are offering these, you also have to calculate the production costs and logistics carefully.

The next step is to create lots of marketing materials. This might be video trailers for your project, special images, flyers and all kinds of communication which will help explain your project clearly to potential backers. Your passion for your project must be present at all times so your enthusiasm is infectious. Once your campaign goes live, you will need lots of content to capture people's imagination. A Kickstarter campaign lasts, on average, for 30 days, and for all of that time you will want to be busy, reaching out to people and attracting attention to your project. You will be busy answering questions and doing publicity and engaging with your audience, so you need to prepare as much material in advance as possible.

Everything you produce must be incredibly clear and accessible to people from all over the world. If you describe something in a way someone might misunderstand, it could cause major problems for you later if you have accidentally promised something you can't deliver; so make sure you have people proofread everything from lots of perspectives. Even if your text is a bit ambiguous or your message is slightly confusing, you might end up wasting lots of time explaining that element to people.

If it's your first time running a Kickstarter or crowdfunding project, don't do it alone. It will be very hard work and it's easy to miss simple errors or oversights if you're the only person looking at the project. Involve friends and experienced people and share the work. Collaboration always makes things better. Surround yourself with experts you can trust, who will believe in your dream with you and offer constructive criticism in a supportive way to help you make it the best it can be.

When your Kickstarter campaign is running, if things are going well, you will see your number of backers gradually growing and your finances slowly creeping towards your goal. With Kickstarter, until the campaign ends, those backers can still pull out, or at the last minute, their credit card might fail. So ideally, you should be aiming to raise more than your minimum goal before the deadline.

Once your campaign is successful, you have to produce everything and keep your backers updated with any news along the way. As you can see, it's a very complex adventure and many people have made mistakes that have cost them a lot — for example, underestimating shipping costs could end up costing you because you are committed to [delivering]

Page Left: *Oracularium*, Aste, A. and Kelso, N.

everything. There are lots of risks, but if you manage your campaign carefully, there are also great rewards waiting for you.

What did you find satisfying about the Kickstarter method of publishing?

It's very satisfying to work directly with customers who are often just as excited about the product as you are! They are part of the journey too, which is very special.

What difficulties or obstacles did you come up against during the process?

It can be incredibly mentally demanding to run a Kickstarter campaign. Checking the numbers can be very depressing and concerning at times. It can cause you to panic and try to implement new strategies. Even when things are going well, it can be unsettling if you don't know why there was a sudden jump up or down.

It's also important to remember that you're connecting with people online, and some people behave in very unusual or sometimes rude or unthinking ways. An offhand comment can be very damaging and hurtful. You have put your 'baby' out there to be judged and that can leave you feeling very vulnerable, so do everything you can to be resilient and prepare for the negativity, as well as the overwhelming compliments.

Is it possible to make a profit from a Kickstarter?

Yes, it's possible to make a profit from Kickstarter, but it's very unpredictable. If your main object is to make lots of money easily, it's not the right path for you. The projects that do really well have both an excellent concept, which has been well articulated, and a lot of luck, often reaching the right audience at the right time. Your focus, when you approach Kickstarter, should be entirely directed towards creating something wonderful and doing everything you can to support it. Ultimately, the overall success and profitability is outside your control. It's not about how much money you make, it's about seeing your dreams come true, step by step. If you do your homework, that dream will come true and, if you're lucky, maybe you'll make some money along the way too.

What advice would you give anyone who is considering launching a Kickstarter campaign for their deck?

Study Kickstarter inside-out. Back some projects and look for best practice. Assemble a team who are experts in every field - if you try to wear too many hats, the whole process is overwhelming. To give you some context, *The Book of Shadows* and *Oracolarium* were very big projects that we had worked on for over 3 years prior to launching our Kickstarter campaign. No doubt, simpler projects could happen faster, but don't trap yourself with unrealistic deadlines by underestimating the amount of work you'll need to do your idea justice.

USING PRINTING COMPANIES

Not every printing company will be right for every creator, so some research is advisable. Other creators will be happy to share their experience with their printers, and there are brokers who will be able to find the best fit for your deck and the experience you are looking for.

Lina Chen, who works for both Shenzhen The Wheel of Fortune Spiritual Art Creation Co. Ltd and Shenzhen XM Playing Cards Co. Ltd, follows a set routine with all of her customers. This will begin with initial communication and then a quotation. Samples of existing cards (but not full decks) can be sent for the customer to check card stock and quality but will require a delivery cost of $30.

Should you wish to proceed, the design files are then sent to, and will be confirmed by, the printer. Design files, which should be in PDF format, must be 300DPI (dots per inch) and in CMYK color (the standard color type for printing, as opposed to RGB which is specifically for screen usage). In terms of this particular printing company, 30% of the payment is expected before mass production and the remaining 70% must be paid before shipment.

The minimum quantity of decks that Shenzhen will print is 500. It usually takes between 4-8 days for the files to be confirmed and then 25-45 days for full production. The delivery lead time is 23-45 days, depending on whether the shipping is by sea or air. Once the shipment has been received, the printer then deals with feedback from the customer. Aftercare is provided, and Shenzhen will take responsibility for any quality problems from their side. In order for a safe delivery, they shrink-wrap and bubble-wrap each deck for protection and use two cartons to hold the load. A website also provides a tracking number, inventory and costs.

Shenzhen prides itself in keeping the customer happy and being up to date with the newest features available in printing. Their box designs range from standard lift-off lids to circular containers, as well as book-shaped boxes that open from a spine. They are also experts at foiling, using a range of metallic colors, embossing, and edging.

PRINT-ON-DEMAND

Printing companies often have a minimum quantity required to print a batch of cards — and this can mean a sizable investment from the creator before they sell a single unit. Because of this, printing can become expensive and therefore unfeasible for some creators. Putting money into a new project such as this is a risk, because even though market research might appear to be positive, attitudes can change and not everyone who says they are interested in a copy will eventually part with their cash. One way of getting around this problem is to use on-demand printing.

Most of the well-known on-demand printing services available are based online, where your card images can be uploaded and built into a deck. Once an account has been registered, you are pretty much 'good to go' and can begin designing. There are often many different features to help you customize your pack. What you choose — such as card size, cardstock, and quantity – will affect the price. Options for packaging — whether you would like a simple tuck box, one with a window, or a clear plastic case — will also affect the final unit cost. These are all determined at the outset, before you even upload your card images, but the specifics can be altered or erased throughout the process. You are not expected to pay a thing until you order your creation.

Printer Studio (which also specializes in making personalized greeting cards, games, and clothing) is used by many card creators due to their efficiency, quality, and how easy their site is to navigate. Once you have registered and logged your specifics, it really is as easy as uploading your images and dropping them into a card frame template. For the novice, guidelines are indicated, and the customer is carefully taken through the procedure. Images can still be manipulated to some extent (turning them sepia, for example), titles can be added, and there is even the option to include your own back design. However, the card sizes offered are preset and not adjustable, so you'll need to ensure that your artwork fits the correct dimensions, or parts of your illustration will be cropped away when printed.

What makes on-demand printing attractive to many is its ability to turn paintings on canvas or digital files from your computer into a physical deck of cards. Some people will only want a copy for themselves (and maybe a few extra for friends), and this method of printing provides a product that looks professional but doesn't break the bank. The more copies you buy, the lower the unit cost becomes, but even one copy, depending on specifications, will be within the price range of a mass-market tarot deck.

Printer Studio also offers the user the option of a marketplace to sell their products. For someone who does not wish to deal with the administration and mailing of decks to the customer, this is all taken care of: you simply set the price per unit, taking into account how much profit you think is reasonable after Printer Studio has taken their cut for printing, postage, and packing.

Alexandre Musruck
Creator of *The Enchanted Journey Lenormand Oracle*

What inspired you to create decks?

I never intended to become a deck creator, let alone [to sell] them. I first attempted to create a Lenormand deck because I wanted something that would reflect who I am and what I like. I desired something that was vintage, chic, and elegant, so I created *Mon Petit Lenormand.* When I posted pictures of the deck and used it on my YouTube videos, people started to ask questions about it, wanting to know who the creator was. When I told them I had created it myself, they asked if they could buy it and so I decided to try and sell. I then caught the deck creator bug. My creations eventually found an audience.

Why did you initially choose to print your decks through on-demand printers?

I chose on-demand printing services because there is no minimum amount required for ordering; you can print just a single deck if you want to. Many printers request a minimum of 500 copies to take your work and when you have a big amount to sell, you also need a lot of space to store your products. I had previously created 500 decks (the *Mon Petit Lenormand,* which was my first Lenormand) in this way. The island I live on imposes a special tax called *L'octroi de mer,* which is applied to any imported products from foreign countries. This makes the selling price of the product go up. On-demand printers do offer the choice of a marketplace where they will sell the product on their platform for you, or orders that you place can be shipped directly to your client. Obviously, this option works better for my customers and me.

What is the process of printing in this way?

After my art is created, I upload the images to the website and order the first copy as a test run. This is to see if the final product meets with my expectations and [if] I also like to work with them in my readings. It is important to see if the deck works or if any improvements need to be made. Once that is done, I place it on my website and inform the public that a new deck is available for sale.

The interface on the printer's website is user-friendly. They offer templates to help you get the right dimension and everything you need to know is explained properly.

2

What difficulties have you encountered with on-demand printing?

I have never met with any difficulties in using on-demand printers.

Can you make a profit from selling decks in this way?

Yes. As with any type of business, selling a deck in this way does allow for the creator to make a profit. However, it is important to understand that creating a deck takes a lot of time and effort. I have had many sleepless nights with some of my creations.

How does the pricing and cost of posting work when selling on-demand decks?

Many things must be taken into consideration when pricing a deck; the amount of effort put into the making of it, for starters. Sometimes, there are additional costs, such as the writing and designing of a guide or companion book. Unfortunately, I will never be able to offer the same price as a mass-market publisher. For example, the *Alexandre Musruck Lenormand Oracle Cards* (published by Red Feather, Schiffer) retails at $14.99. When I initially self-published this deck (originally named *Classic Lenormand*) I had to sell it at 25€, which is nearly $30. I cannot afford to buy the thousands of decks that Schiffer can. In the printing industry, the more you buy, the less you pay, which cuts the cost for the customer.

Which on-demand printers would you recommend?

I've used different on-demand and bulk printers during a decade of creating and printing decks. I mostly work with Printer Studio. They offer professional quality printing [and] good cardstock (from standard to linen, as well as 100% plastic). There are many different sizes to choose from too, depending on your project. They have always been professional and replied promptly to any inquiries I have had.

What is the most satisfying part of creating a deck?

The most satisfying part of the whole experience is having control of my work the printing process as well as the financial aspects. Creating your own brand and products is a good experience and it's empowering. It might not be enough to make a full living from but it's a great adventure. For anyone who wants to print their decks and offer them to the public, I would highly encourage them to do so!

Page Right: *The Enchanted Journey Lenormand Cards*, Musruck, A

24

HOME PRINTING

Even though there are premium models on the market, it is still possible to create high-quality prints at home, even with a modest home printer. The major advantage to this method is timing, since you really can, if you desire, create and print out your own deck relatively quickly. I have made simple but professional-looking oracles, comprising 40 or 50 cards, in a day. This is great if you're just producing a deck for your own personal use. For those considering other routes of printing or publication, you can always create a dummy deck on a home printer, allowing you to test it out before taking the plunge and contacting a publishing house or printing company.

Home printing will likely require more than just a printer, though. You'll need to size your cards and ensure they all fit together, so a program like Photoshop or Adobe InDesign will help you with this. If you're replicating physical artwork (like collage), then you can scan it in before printing, meaning you'll probably still need to use a program to lay it out and ensure everything is the right size. Then you'll be able to print multiples to a page (thereby saving materials) and add titles to each card.

You can print your cards in a variety of different 'weights' (which refers to how thick, or heavy, the paper or card you choose is), but I have found — especially with small, poker-size decks — that photo-paper or a thin card (specific for printing) will work well when laminated. The larger the finished card dimensions, the thinner it will appear. Home laminators with a heat setting will keep your printed cards clean and giving them a professional sheen.

Page Right: Photography by May, L. Cards from *The New Chapter Tarot*. Briggs, K.

PUBLICISING YOUR ORACLE

If you are considering selling your deck, then publicity and marketing are of great importance. Many wonderful decks have been less successful than they ought to have been because they weren't advertised particularly well. An oracle or tarot deck is only as successful as the publicity machine behind it, so once you have something to show, it's a good idea to find ways in which you can build a relationship with those who might be interested in buying it.

SOCIAL MEDIA

Social media is, undeniably, one of the most effective tools for publicizing a deck. It provides multiple platforms through which creators are able to show off their work, not only to prospective customers, but to publishers who may be on the lookout for new and exciting acquisition possibilities.

INSTAGRAM

Instagram is probably one of the most recognizable platforms for visual arts since it revolves almost exclusively around images. Because of this, Instagram hosts a huge community of tarot readers, and many enjoy seeing the process of a deck being created — not just the finished product. It's a good idea to create an account (if you haven't already) while you're still creating the deck. You can upload individual cards and drum up anticipation and a following in the run-up to publication. This can help you to gauge which printing option is right for you — and because publishers use Instagram to find prospective decks, you may even get an offer before your deck is complete!

You can either upload previews of your progress to your own account or create another one specifically for your project. This might attract a bigger crowd, unless you already have a large following, in which case your personal account might get more reach. When creating a name for the deck's account, keep it as close to the title of your deck as possible. If you want people to find your work, then it will need to be easy to search for. A profile photo should carry an image of your product or some kind of recognizable logo. Your profile is important and needs to show, in a nutshell, what you offer.

THERE ARE MANY THINGS TO CONSIDER WHEN USING INSTAGRAM...

1. Post regularly. The advice for Instagram has remained consistent since the platform was launched, and that is to post as regularly as possible. Of course, that's not to say you should flood your feed: you will want to keep your audience updated with new pieces of work and information about your deck, but too many posts can be irritating and could put people off. Don't post more than once per day. Posting daily will increase your reach (how many people see your post), but if you don't have the content for daily posts, just post as often as you can. Wednesday to Friday are the best days to post, and social media analysis companies say that 10am-3pm are the best hours to post.

2. Use relevant hashtags. Hashtags can be a great way of generating interest in your deck. However, it is not about using as many as you can (30 being the current limit); rather, it is about being specific and finding the right hashtags for your posts. While #tarot and #oraclecards will be obvious suggestions, think about the theme of your deck and the way in which is created. If you are a digital artist, then consider the tools you are using. Hashtags like #procreate, #photoshopartist or #penandink could increase your audience. An Instagram post will receive 12.6% more interest when you include one hashtag with your post.

3. Follow others. It can pay to follow others; not only because it can be inspiring and make the whole process more enjoyable, but because it is a great way of making contact with other creators or those who will gladly endorse your deck. Commenting on other people's posts is an easy way of interacting with the oracle community and can build real relationships with those who might want to buy your finished product.

4. Consider a theme. Many Instagram accounts have themes. This is often built around a pallet or style, meaning that the feed appears consistent and considered. A theme can add a professional look to your deck account and make it stand out amongst the crowd. For example, should your deck have a pastel palette, might you translate this into your theme, and use a similar font throughout?

5. Be original. The more interesting a photo is, the more likely someone will be to follow you. Rather than just uploading pictures of your cards, think about how they are presented. Do you choose to show a detail of the card instead of the whole thing? Might you show cards being used on a table from above? The setup of the table and background is just as important. People like to imagine using the cards themselves and this will allow them to see your deck in action and put themselves in the position of the reader. Adding your hands to the photographs, showing the cards in a real reading and their size, is an effective marketing tool. Posts receive 38% more likes when a person or face is included

in a picture so think about how you set up your visual posts. A selfie with your deck might bring a more human element to your feed than just the illustrations. People often like to see the face behind the cards.

6. Be engaging. You might think that Instagram is all about the pictures, but this is not necessarily true. What is written explains what is happening in the photographs. This is the perfect opportunity to explain aspects of your deck or update readers about new developments but it can also be a creative opportunity too. You may wish to speak about what inspired a certain card or even engage with your followers. Engagement is a very important metric on social media. Any interaction with a post counts towards its 'engagement', so you'll want to encourage your followers to comment, share, etc. This can be achieved through simple 'calls to action', like asking your followers about their own experiences with tarot, for example, what a certain card means to them.

7. Use Stories. Instagram's Stories feature is really worth using. Appearing at the top of the timeline, you can upload multiple Stories a day. These posts tend to be more lighthearted than the glossy photos that will populate your main feed. You can invite questions, post quizzes, or share other people's posts to your Stories. Many people use it as a peek behind the curtain, giving little insights on a project's process, or simply sharing a fun moment from their day.

8. Don't be a salesperson. Nobody wants to feel as though they are being targeted or pushed to buy something. Instagram accounts that do well tend to be very authentic — the platform is all about getting a glimpse into someone's life, so remember that this account is your place to genuinely share the creative process. You can be enthusiastic about it, and you'll definitely want to tell your followers how they can buy your deck. But approach it from a personal level, rather than a sales point of view, and you'll get a much better response.

Accounts to follow: @indiedeckreview @tatiannatarot @biddytarot @littleredtarot

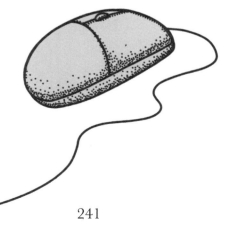

241

Page Right: *Modern Witch Tarot*, Sterle, L. (This is also a self-portrait of the artist!)

FACEBOOK

Because most people are on Facebook, it continues to be a good platform for sharing your projects. But although your friends and family will be excited about your new project, they might not necessarily want to receive regular updates. An independent Facebook Page can be set up for your deck, so that people can follow your progress there; these posts will still appear on their newsfeed. You can include images, videos, and even have the ability to speak live to your followers. It is important to have a base where people can find you, and a Facebook Page, like an Instagram account, is an easy and free way of achieving this.

Facebook also allows users to create Groups. A Group is a secure place where a creator can share and discuss topics with their members. It is private and the host is in charge of who can join. If you are just beginning to create a deck, then this might be a useful place to assemble those you respect and seek opinions about your work in a controlled environment. Some creators will bring together others from the industry to test out their ideas or images, but most will use the Group function as a way of keeping prospective customers updated of their progress.

TWITTER

Twitter has much the same purpose as Instagram and Facebook, though it is better as a tool for short updates and communication. Just like Instagram, there is a large tarot community on Twitter, so it's worth finding some accounts to follow and engaging with posts other than your own in order to really interact with the community. Retweeting other people's posts is another great way to engage, so look for ones that fit your deck's theme or general vibe.

Unlike Facebook Groups, anyone can comment on your Twitter posts, which is something to think about before setting up an account for your work. Not all opinions will be welcome and while the platform could provide a wide reach, Twitter is well known for having incendiary discussions. Keep away from contentious topics though, and you should be fine!

Accounts to follow: @thetarotlady @treadwells @witcheshotline @thejessicadore

MIND, BODY & SPIRIT SUPPLIERS

Local businesses can be a good option for seeking local interest and sales. If you have a local Mind, Body & Spirit store, this could be a good place to display or sell your deck. A smaller shop might be interested in selling signed copies of your deck or might even organize a 'meet and greet' so that you can interact with their customers. Some like to have their deck signed in person, and this is a good opportunity to provide the occasional reading, using your deck, for promotional purposes.

YOUTUBE

YouTube has a vast and developing oracle and tarot community. It is a great place for publicizing new decks, and you needn't always have a channel yourself to take advantage of it. There are many established YouTubers who would be happy to showcase your deck by walking through the cards one by one, reviewing it, or even interviewing you about your work. There will be those who will buy your deck and do this voluntarily, but it makes sense to seek out a few you like and ask if they'd be interested in making a video in exchange for a review copy. Many tarot or oracle deck enthusiasts will jump at the chance and receiving a deck ahead of a release date, if possible, gives them an exclusive for their channel and means that you get extra publicity.

Before you submit anything to anyone, take a look at a variety of channels and see which presenter's style would suit your deck. Some will give only their first impressions (known as an 'unboxing') but there are others who enjoy a deeper look, reading the accompanying book and bonding with a deck of cards before they record a review. Of course, there is no reason why you cannot take advantage of both kinds of endorsement.

Accounts to follow: Ethony, FablesDen, TarotOracle, BiddyTarot

MAILING LISTS

Mailing lists are not as prevalent as they once were but many established tarot and oracle creators still use newsletters to keep their fans and customers up to date with what they're producing. Not everyone uses social media, and a link to a mailing list can usually be added to a creator's website. As with other internet resources, it is important to remain consistent but to not overshare. People will be happy to receive regular and informative emails but will unsubscribe if they feel as though they are being contacted too often.

WEBSITE

Many creators already have a website and, should this be the case, a page can be added to an existing site to publicize your deck. If your website is tarot- or oracle-related, then this will make perfect sense. However, if it is not, you might want to build a second website for your creation. It is worth remembering that this will cost and take a substantial amount of time, effort and knowhow. There are companies that you can pay to host your site — SquareSpace, for example, offers hosting and also gives you the tools you need to build your perfect website. Other companies, like Wix, do the same but will add their own URL to yours unless you pay to upgrade to a unique URL.

If you intend to create more than one deck, then it might be sensible to create a site that houses all of them rather than just one for an individual set. Try to choose a name that directly focuses on your deck and keep it as simple as possible.

FAIRS AND CONFERENCES

New Age fairs prove to be a popular place for both the selling and promotion of decks. You'll need to apply to have a table, and this will cost you some money, but it's often worthwhile for the exposure that the fair will offer you. People enjoy meeting a creator in person, and this could drive interest in your deck. If you are attending a fair, don't forget to promote on social media first, so that people know where you are going to be.

A conference is not unlike a fair but is usually refined in its focus. The UK Tarot Conference, run by Kim Arnold, is the biggest of its kind in the United Kingdom and has been running for seventeen years. Its presenters have included some of the biggest authors, artists and creators from within the world of tarot and oracle. As well as its key speakers, the three-day conference also welcomes creators who might wish to promote their deck and offers space for sellers. The conference's younger sibling, The London Tarot Festival, is a one-day event, providing the same features on a smaller scale. Respected names within the field, such as Liz Dean, Tori Hartman, Janet Piedilato and Philip and Stephanie Carr-Gomm, have all presented their creations at one of these events. Again, you will need to apply to the organizers to get a table or speak at these events. All information about this is available on their websites.

MAGAZINES

Magazines are another useful marketing opportunity. As the founder *The Esotoracle*, I am aware of the exposure such magazines can offer to creators, since ours is distributed worldwide. We have our own section, titled Preview, which lists up-and-coming decks for the next season, showcasing a selection of mass-market and self-published tarots and oracles.

With *The Esotoracle* in mind, we are always happy to profile new releases and, on occasion, add one to our cover. We are glad to include new voices from the tarot and oracle world to our publication, and those with a new title are often thrilled to have their work displayed in print.

The Esotoracle is not the only tarot and oracle magazine on the market and there are many other esoteric and New Age publications available. Flip through a few and see how they promote new decks. A simple email could bag you an interview, article, or a place amongst their new releases. When the *Spirit Within Tarot* was released, I was a guest diviner for *Take a Break: Fate & Fortune Magazine*, pulling a card for each of the zodiac signs during April. A little later, I wrote a three-page article about the deck in Watkins' *Mind, Body and Spirit Magazine* and had my deck featured in *Kindred Spirit Magazine*. As you can imagine, being featured in these magazines really helped boost my deck's sales.

INFLUENCERS

An 'influencer' is the term given to someone who might successfully influence others to buy your deck. As already discussed, there are many YouTubers who will be happy to review your work, but this is also true of those on Instagram. If you think someone with a large following might show off your work to great effect, it could be prudent to ask if they'd like to receive a sample copy for the purpose.

Word of mouth is a powerful way of passing on information, and there are many prominent members of the tarot and oracle industry whose names will open doors. Prior to printing, it is a good idea to seek out those you admire and ask if they would be interested in providing a short recommendation about your deck; a quote that can be printed directly onto the packaging. If the deck is yet to be printed, then most will accept a selection of digital images, an overview of your intentions, and a sample of text from your manual.

Once printed, you might want to send a copy to those who you feel would add weight to your product. However, here is a cautionary tip: I am aware of many high-profile authors who have been sent a deck, or have received emails from those who expect them to endorse a product, *without being asked first*. If you are going to contact anyone in the hope that they'll publicize your work, show some respect and let them know how much you would appreciate their help. Some courtesy goes a long way, and good contacts will last you a lifetime!

THINK OUTSIDE THE BOX

Try to be as open to new ideas as you can. There are many obvious routes to take, but your individuality could bring about unexpected results. For example, should you have created an oracle based around plants, a garden or flower show might be as good a place to promote your deck as a New Age fair.

CONCLUSION

Creating a deck, whether an oracle or tarot, can be one of the most rewarding things that you will do. From my own experience, having tried to create a deck for many years before I actually completed one, it was like crossing a line. Once I knew I had completed my first, I knew I could do it again. Andrea Aste compares the new deck to a baby, and, in some ways, it is — a new life that we nurture, and which holds so much of our own experience and spiritual DNA.

I have tried to give as many helpful tips as I can in this book, drawing on the tried-and-tested experience of friends within the industry who have encountered parts of this process that I have not. I hope that this book acts as both an inspirational resource for those who wish to create their own 'baby', and as a guide for those creators who wish to know a little more about the world of publishing and printing their own work.

The next step is up to you. With this information under your belt and your own creativity ready to be unleashed, the adventure is only just beginning. We all have a story to tell. What will yours be, and how will you choose to tell it?

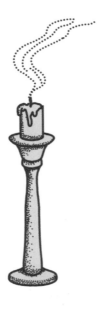

·ᴥᴥ· Acknowledgments ·ᴥᴥ·

Author's Note

I would like to thank all the talented artists who contributed images to this book, as well as the creators who offered their insights in the form of interviews. I would like to also thank everyone at Liminal 11 for their expertise, and my partner, Daz, for his continued support.

Image Credits

Photography & In-House Credits